Before Beveridge:
Welfare Before the Welfare State

The IEA Health and Welfare Unit

Choice in Welfare No. 47

Before Beveridge:
Welfare Before the Welfare State

David Gladstone (Editor)
David G. Green
Jose Harris
Jane Lewis
Pat Thane
A.W. Vincent
Noel Whiteside

IEA Health and Welfare Unit
London

First published January 1999

The IEA Health and Welfare Unit
2 Lord North St
London SW1P 3LB

'Political Thought and the Welfare State 1870-1940: An Intellectual Framework for British Social Policy', by Jose Harris was first published in *Past and Present*, Vol. 135, May 1992 and is reproduced here by permission.

'The Working Class and State "Welfare" in Britain, 1880-1914', by Pat Thane was first published in *The Historical Journal*, Vol. 27, No. 4, 1984 and is reproduced here by permission.

'The Poor Law Reports of 1909 and the Social Theory of the Charity Organisation Society', by A.W. Vincent was first published in *Victorian Studies*, Vol. 27, No. 3, Spring 1984 and is reproduced here by permission.

Front cover: cartoon of William Beveridge by Low, image supplied by the National Portrait Gallery, London, © Solo Syndication Ltd.

ISBN 0-255 36439-3
ISSN 1362-9565

Typeset by the IEA Health and Welfare Unit
in Bookman 10 point
Printed in Great Britain by
The Cromwell Press
Trowbridge, Wiltshire

Contents

The Authors

David Gladstone is Director of Studies in Social Policy in the School for Policy Studies at the University of Bristol. He has published extensively on British social policy past and present. He edited *British Social Welfare: Past, Present and Future*, UCL Press 1995 and his history of the twentieth century welfare state is forthcoming from Macmillan. In addition, David Gladstone is General Series Editor of Historical Sources in Social Welfare, Routledge/Thoemmes Press, and of the Open University Press' Introducing Social Policy Series. David Gladstone lectures widely on aspects of British welfare history and has held several Visiting Professorships, especially in the USA.

David G. Green is the Director of the Health and Welfare Unit at the Institute of Economic Affairs. His books include *Power and Party in an English City*, Allen & Unwin, 1980; *Mutual Aid or Welfare State*, Allen & Unwin, 1984 (with L. Cromwell); *Working Class Patients and the Medical Establishment*, Temple Smith/ Gower, 1985; and *The New Right: The Counter Revolution in Political, Economic and Social Thought*, Wheatsheaf, 1987; *Reinventing Civil Society*, 1993; and *Community Without Politics*, 1996. He wrote the chapter on 'The Neo-Liberal Perspective' in *The Student's Companion to Social Policy*, Blackwell, 1998.

Jose Harris is Professor of Modern History in the University of Oxford, and currently holds a Leverhulme Research Professorship. An extensively revised second edition of her *William Beveridge: an Autobiography* was published in 1997.

Jane Lewis is a Fellow of All Souls College, Oxford and Director of the Wellcome Unit for the History of Medicine. She will shortly be moving to the University of Nottingham. She is the author of *The Voluntary Sector, the State and Social Work in Britain*, 1995, as well as numerous books and articles on gender and social policy, and health and community care. Most recently she has published, with K. Kiernan and H. Land, *Lone Motherhood in Twentieth Century Britain*, 1998.

Pat Thane is Professor of Contemporary History at the University of Sussex. She is the author of *Foundations of the Welfare State*, Longmans, second edition 1996 and of numerous articles on the history of social welfare and of women. She is currently completing a book on the history of old age in England for Oxford University Press.

Andrew Vincent is Professor of Political Theory, School of European Studies, University of Wales, Cardiff and Associate Editor of the *Journal of Political Ideologies*. He was formerly a Fellow at the Research School of the Social Sciences, Australian National University. Recent books include *Theories of the State*, 1994 reprint; *Modern Political Ideologies*, second edition 1995; *A Radical Hegelian: The Political and Social Philosophy of Henry Jones*, with David Boucher, 1993; and (ed.) *Political Theory: Tradition and Diversity*, 1997. He is currently completing a book on twentieth-century political theory.

Noel Whiteside is Reader in Public Policy at the School for Policy Studies, University of Bristol. She formerly worked as Research Fellow at the Centre for Social History at Warwick University and at the Public Records Office in London. She has published a number of books and articles on employment change and social policy in historical and comparative perspective, also on the mixed economy of welfare. Recent books include *Bad Times: Unemployment in British Social and Political History*, 1991; *Aux Sources du Chomage: France - Grande Bretagne 1880-1914*, edited with M. Mansfield and R. Salais, 1994; *Governance, Industry and Labour Markets in Britain and France*, edited with R. Salais, 1998. She is currently researching comparisons in recent labour market change and systems of social protection in Britain, France and Germany.

Editor's Introduction
Welfare Before the Welfare State

David Gladstone

M UCH of the discussion following the Cabinet changes in July
1998 centred on the future of welfare reform. One view
argued, especially with the resignation of Frank Field from his
specifically designated post of Minister for Welfare Reform, that
'thinking the unthinkable' was no longer on the agenda, and that
radical change to Britain's welfare state was no longer a priority
of the Blair government. A contrary view asserted that, despite
the change in personnel at the Department of Social Security, the
project remained in place; and that, with Alasdair Darling as the
new Social Security Secretary of State, there would be a greater
emphasis on the delivery of welfare change.

There are certainly indicators which suggest the continuity
rather than abandonment of the agenda of welfare reform. The
raft of reviews initiated in the first year of the Blair government
remain in place, such as the important review of pensions, for
example; and 'welfare to work' remains an on-going feature of
political rhetoric. In that context it is at least feasible to suggest
that radical alternatives challenging dependency on the welfare
state that were once the preserve of the political Right remain the
established (though politically conflictual) language of the Blairite
project. Such an interpretation summons up a vision of the
welfare state leaner and fitter for the twenty-first century. But, in
some respects at least, it represents a re-configuration of an
earlier experience of welfare; the vision is of welfare before the
welfare state. It is the contemporary debate about the future of
welfare that gives these historical essays a timely appeal and
significance.

While a growing consensus seems to have emerged among
British politicians that Britain's welfare state is in need of radical
restructuring, historians have become more comprehensive in
their exploration of Britain's welfare past. Earlier studies
published in the 1960s and 1970s, as Lewis notes in this

1

volume, tended to focus almost exclusively on the role of the state and to stress the eventual triumph of collectivism over individualism (p. 10). Titles such as *The Coming of the Welfare State* or *The Evolution of the British Welfare State* tended to emphasise what Finlayson graphically termed 'the welfare state escalator'[1] in which Britain emerged 'from the darkness of the nineteenth- century poor law into the light of the Beveridge Plan of 1942 and the post-war welfare state' (p. 10).

A recent commentator has noted that the 'benefit of the political developments of the 1980s and 1990s to historians ... is that the challenge to the welfare state has led to the death of teleological interpretations and produced a much greater sensitivity to the wide range of possibilities in coping with risks in society'.[2] This greater sensitivity has centred around the mixed economy of welfare—the recognition of that complex patterning of formal and informal agencies and institutions providing some security against the threats to welfare. In the past—as well as the present—the mixed-economy perspective has encompassed the role of the family in financial assistance as well as tending care, the formal voluntary sector combining the earlier traditions of philanthropic benevolence and mutual aid, the commercial market as well as the welfare services delivered by the central and local state. The mixed economy perspective thus recognises the diversity of agencies involved in welfare activity of which the state is only one. It also acknowledges, however, that over the twentieth century the growing role of government has impinged upon and, to some degree at least, redefined the role of each of the other participants in the welfare relationship. In this respect the ambivalence of the voluntary sector in the years between 1945 and 1960 is instructive; so too is the stimulus given by government incentive to the private pensions industry in the 1980s.

As these examples illustrate, the study of the past of welfare has become more complex and comprehensive, as well as more dynamic. The relationships between each of the sectors in the mixed economy have been fluid and changing over time, constituting in Finlayson's terms 'a moving frontier'[3] not only between state and citizen but between the diverse components of the British welfare system itself.

For much of the present century, however, the position and role of the state has become more central. That applies not only to the direct supply of welfare but also to the state's role in subsidising the welfare activities of other sectors (such as the voluntary and commercial sectors or what is now termed the independent sector) and regulating welfare activities by means of an increasingly complex and controlling system of governance.[4] There is little doubt, however, as Harris notes in her essay in this volume, that to a nineteenth century social analyst the preponderance of the state a century later would have appeared surprising. There was a much greater likelihood that 'the provision of social welfare in Britain ... would continue to be highly localised, amateur, voluntaristic and intimate in scale' (p. 43). Within the framework of the mixed economy of welfare, therefore, the historian's task is also to account for the growing role of government and the change, over a comparatively short period of time, to what Harris characterises as 'one of the most uniform, centralised, bureaucratic and "public" welfare systems in Europe and indeed in the modern world' (p. 43). Several of the essays in this collection indicate some facets of explanation but, as, Baldwin notes, so extensive is the literature on the origin, rise and development of the welfare state that 'even the seasoned observer may be forgiven for occasionally feeling lost in the academic Babel of paradigms, models, interpretations and accounts'.[5]

There is more general agreement, however, that the legislation of the years 1944 to 1948—the Education Act 1944, the National Health Service Act 1946, the National Insurance Act 1946 and the National Assistance Act 1948—represented the defining moment in the transition from a residual to an institutional welfare state.[6] It was a time when 'the idea of a residual welfare state that would merely respond to economic and social problems was replaced by a comprehensive welfare ideology in which public social expenditure could be used to change and improve society'.[7] Though the legislation of the 1940s may have constituted a defining moment in welfare collectivism, much recent research has emphasised the continuities between the creation of the classic welfare state and earlier developments:

> Almost all the ideas and proposals for reform in social security and education, for example, had been long discussed in the 1920s and 1930s. The new structures built on or simplified many of the systems that preceded them. In many cases they extended to a national scale experiments which had been introduced by some local authorities.[8]

Health care provides another example. During the 1930s both the British Medical Association and the Socialist Medical

Association set out proposals designed to extend the health care coverage of the population: the former advocating the extension of the insurance scheme introduced in 1911, the latter local authority control. Meanwhile, the tripartite structure for the National Health Service created in 1946 neatly coincided with 'the three nuclei around which health care institutions had aggregated in the course of the previous century'. In this respect 'although widely portrayed as a revolutionary departure, the National Health Service as a mechanism was in most respects evolutionary or even traditional'.[9] Continuity as well as change is thus an important facet in the understanding of Britain's welfare past.

The essays in this collection reflect that emphasis on continuity and change. They cover the years between 1870 and 1940, years during which a considerable structural transformation occurred in British welfare arrangements. The 'moving frontier' and the increasing intervention of the central and local state are thus also integral to their narrative. Three of the essays (Green, Lewis and Whiteside) are principally concerned with agencies and institutions of welfare, specifically the Friendly Societies and the voluntary sector. The essays by Harris, Thane and Vincent explore the dynamic of the debate about welfare that occurred in this period and the reaction of the working class to the increase in state welfare.

At the beginning of the period covered in this collection, the poor law, public health and education all attested to the growing intervention of the state in social welfare. This nineteenth century 'revolution in government' has been portrayed by historians as 'a self-expanding administrative process which, acquiring its own momentum, carried state intervention forward despite ideological and political resistance through the middle years of the nineteenth century'.[10] Yet despite the evidence of the encroaching state, even at the end of the nineteenth century Britain had a small central bureaucracy, and much of the supply of publicly provided welfare was, as Jane Lewis notes, in the hands of local administrators such as poor law guardians and elected school boards (p. 15). Local supply persisted and, indeed, expanded in certain sectors throughout the period between 1870 and 1940, but it did so within the parameters of a more proactive central state. Government bureaucracy expanded, new central government departments were created, the volume of social legislation increased and central government's share of local authority revenue grew. All of this betokened the administrative momentum of a twentieth century revolution in government in which a higher political priority was accorded to welfare issues or what, in nineteenth century parlance, would have been termed 'the condition of the people'. Its effect was a move away from the view that the corporate life of society was expressed through voluntary organisations and the local community to an increasing expectation of the state in terms both of provision and funding. The impact of that transition is an important feature of the 'moving frontier' and in this collection it is discussed by Jane Lewis in a century-long review of the voluntary sector and by David Green and Noel Whiteside who focus upon the friendly societies.

At the end of the nineteenth century, friendly societies were 'the largest exclusively working class organisation in Britain'.[11] In return for the payment of a weekly contribution, the societies offered sickness benefit and the services of a doctor as well as payment to cover funeral expenses. By the end of the century, some societies were offering an extended sickness benefit which was in effect an old-age pension. In addition, friendly societies provided a sense of membership solidarity through their regular meeting nights. The benefits of friendly society membership, however, were only available to those with sufficiently regular employment and wages high enough to be able to afford the weekly premium. To this extent, 'friendly society membership was the badge of the skilled worker'.[12] Insurance against risks to the stability of the family budget was thus already established among the respectable working class through the institutions of mutual aid. That may have been part of its attraction to Lloyd George in introducing his scheme of National Insurance in 1911, although other factors have been suggested.[13] The legislation introduced a system of financial security (not comprehensive, however) that was based on a contractual entitlement achieved through contributions. It did so by drawing finance from workers and employers without 'the politically unpopular necessity to increase income tax'.[14] As such, 'insurance was the capitalist's answer to the problem of want, and by reducing it insurance covered up what the socialist saw as the root cause of poverty'.[15] The 1911 National Insurance Act was in two parts, dealing respectively with unemployment and health insurance. The essays by Green and Whiteside examine the health insurance role of the friendly societies, the 'approved societies' who administered the scheme from its inception in 1912.

David Green has written extensively on the role of the friendly societies. For him, friendly societies represent an important mechanism by which individuals could maintain independence since they provided 'all the services which enabled people to be self supporting' and thereby prevented recourse to the poor law as well as to charity.[16] Green's argument is that this integral feature of respectable working-class life was subverted by changes introduced into the 1911 National Insurance legislation as it went through Parliament. The British Medical Association and the commercial insurance companies established common cause which put in jeopardy the mutual aid tradition of the friendly societies. On the one hand working-class democratic control was replaced by greater medical professional control; on the other, the commercial insurance companies were given the status of approved societies alongside the mutual aid friendly societies.[17]

Noel Whiteside, much of whose recent research has centred on health insurance between the First and Second World Wars, underlines how in that period central control eroded the autonomy and independence of the societies: 'Constant cuts and rising liabilities took their toll on small, local societies—some of which collapsed under the strain', while the effects of the prolonged inter-war recession 'undermined the principles of social insurance' (p. 31). Her essay also shows how what Green sees as the benefits of mutuality, especially democratic control, were falling into abeyance soon after the passage of the 1911 Act; while by the outbreak of the Second World War the tradition of local participation in society's business was fading 'probably because central regulation throttled the possibility of popular participation' (p. 33).

Daunton has recently suggested that: 'the nature of friendly societies needs more attention as does their gradual demise. There was nothing pre-ordained about their replacement by public bodies'.[18] That, however, is what occurred in 1948. Though insurance remained as the base of the income maintenance system, its administration became part of the nationalisation of Britain's welfare system, just as happened with industries such as coal and steel, for example. Whiteside discusses how the inter-war years again shaped the debate about the future of health insurance and how the Beveridge Report (1942) high-lighted the administrative complexities that the operation of the scheme entailed. But there were those who, to the last, were vocal in their support for the personal service that the insurance agents had given and critical of the centralised administration that would replace it. For Green the eradication of mutual aid meant not only the loss of personal service and the pioneering work of the medical aid societies. It also meant that: 'all alterna-tives to the NHS monolith were excluded ... the final vestiges of competition in the supply of health care were driven out of existence'.[19]

The essays so far considered focus principally on the institu-tions of welfare: the others are concerned with ideas. Jose Harris takes a long time span—from 1870 to 1940—in her quest for an intellectual framework for social policy. Andrew Vincent concen-trates on the Majority and Minority Reports on the Poor Law Commission published in 1909. Pat Thane examines working-class attitudes to state welfare in the formative period between 1880 and the outbreak of the First World War in 1914.

The Royal Commission on the Poor Laws occupies a particular position in the aetiology of the British welfare state. Traditionally it has been taken as symbolic of the ideological divide that existed at the beginning of the century about the causes of poverty and its alleviation and the role of the state in welfare. On the one hand the Majority Report has been portrayed as a defence of individualism and anti-statism, influenced by a static stereotypical image of the role of the Charity Organisation Society(COS). On the other, the Minority Report, drafted by Sidney and Beatrice Webb, has been seen as the way of the future with its network of comprehensive public services available to all in the population, and not simply 'reserved for the poor'. Andrew Vincent challenges this dichotomy. His essay argues that the Reports had more in common than has subse-quently been acknowledged. Stressing the ethical—rather than atomistic—individualism that he believes characterised the Majority Report, he argues that: 'the COS were not, in the 1900s, advocates of individualism in any direct, simple sense'. Mean-while: '[T]he Minority Report was not really so forward looking a document as its supporters have claimed'. For Vincent, it revealed what he describes as 'the less congenial side of the

Webbs' thought: their incurable partiality for élites and for bureaucratic organisation' (p. 85).

Jose Harris explores in some detail the ideas of those affiliated to the Charity Organisation Society and the particular influence on British welfare policy and practice of philosophical Idealism as mediated especially through the writings of Bernard Bosanquet, the COS's social theorist. Like Vincent, she emphasises the diversity of views that had become a feature of the COS by the early twentieth century. By that time 'its leading members had a strong conception of the corporate nature of society and of the organic interdependence of its members' (p. 55) symbolised by Helen Bosanquet's notion of social collectivism. By this term she sought to express 'the companionship and assistance of friendly societies, co-operatives and trade unions' in contrast to 'the barren intercourse with poor law officials'. These ideas found their way into the Majority Report with its emphasis upon a social policy that was 'preventive, curative and restorative' with treatment both 'adapted to the needs of the individual' and designed 'to foster the instincts of independence and self maintenance among those assisted'.[20] Such an analysis of welfare intervention was thus less concerned with the agency by whom it was provided than with the ethical personal relationship which existed between the giver and the recipient, and the supremacy of the aim of promoting independent citizenship in the recipient. Many of their critics were not slow to point out, however, that 'the deviant or needy individual could far more easily be provoked into self-improvement from within the context of state social services than if left to his own unaided efforts' (p. 57).

But what of the working class themselves and their attitudes to the welfare provisions of the expanding state? This is the significance of Pat Thane's essay which highlights three important themes. First, the diversity of views and the difference of opinion that existed among the specifically working-class organisations whose records she has consulted: political, friendly society, trade union, the co-operative movement and trades councils. Secondly, the importance of the distinction within the working class itself between the 'helpable poor' and the residuum. Writing of the Independent Labour Party's programme of social reform she comments that its aim was 'to give maximum aid to the majority of self-respecting, hard-working people whose wages and conditions of life kept them severely deprived despite their best efforts' (p. 103). Supporting independence rather than encouraging dependence was its objective. Thirdly, support for state action in welfare was highly specific. Reforms which entailed sacrifice—such as education—were less popular than those such as old-age pensions which did not. Similarly, there was considerable opposition to 'measures which entailed "intrusion" into working-class lives and homes' (p. 105). The lines appeared to be drawn quite clearly. On the one hand there was 'opposition to state action or to private philanthropy which ... sought to impose standards of behaviour upon the working class', on the other there was 'acceptance of reform which was non-punitive, redistributive and conferred real material improvement' (p. 107). But for all that she concludes that 'very many people would have preferred as an ideal, regular work, wages sufficient for a decent life ... allowing them sufficient surplus to save for hard times'. In this world view there was a minimal role for the state. It lay in providing those services which independent individuals could not provide for themselves and especially for those who were restricted by physical or other factors from achieving an independent existence. Welfare services, therefore, apparently represented a poor substitute for the independence that could be offered by adequately remunerated and regular employment.

In this sense, the parameters of the political debate about welfare appear to show a remarkable tenacity. At the century's end—as at its beginning—the concern is still with state and citizen, bureaucracy and responsiveness, freedom and coercion, work and welfare. To his brief tenure of the position of Minister for Welfare Reform, Frank Field brought an understanding and awareness of earlier forms of welfare supply. It is perhaps appropriate, therefore, that his is the final word.

> Being the costliest part of the government budget, welfare has enormous potential for good or ill. The question is no longer 'does welfare affect values?' but what action should it promote and nurture. When put like this most people would suggest work, savings and honesty and that the greatest of these is work. Just as it is in the shadow of the bay tree that we grow good, so from the protection offered by work, savings and honesty can prosper.[21]

The Voluntary Sector in the Mixed Economy of Welfare

Jane Lewis

The Mixed Economy of Welfare

THE historiography of welfare states has tended to focus almost exclusively on the role of the state and to stress the eventual triumph of collectivism over individualism. Britain, for example, has often been portrayed as emerging from the darkness of the nineteenth-century poor law into the light of the Beveridge Plan of 1942 and the post-war welfare state. This has tended to be a story of linear development and progress. However, rather than seeing the story of the modern welfare state in terms of ever increasing amounts of state intervention, it is more accurate to see modern states as always having had a mixed economy of welfare, in which the state, the voluntary sector, the family and the market have played different parts at different points in time. Indeed, as Paci has noted,[1] it is a major challenge to comparative work on the history of welfare regimes to chart and explain the changing balance between the various elements in the mixed economy. This might have been more obvious to British historians of welfare somewhat earlier if they had engaged in more European comparative research. For example, many European countries have had long experience of the kind of separation of (state) finance from (private and voluntary) provision in the realm of social services, something that has become an explicit policy goal in Britain only since 1988. Any assumption as to incrementalist state intervention was thrown into question during the 1980s by the stated determination of some governments (particularly the British) to reduce the role of the state and the less ideological response of others (for example, the Netherlands) to curb rising public expenditure, especially on social security and health care.

Richard Titmuss[2] sought to remind us that social provision consisted of more than state provision. He identified occupational provision by employers (at a time when occupational pensions were becoming widespread) and fiscal provision through the tax system as also being of crucial importance. However, historically, throughout Europe and in spite of differences, the family has been the largest provider of welfare[3] and its importance in this regard shows no sign of decline (*pace* the analysis of functional sociologists in the 1950s). Within the family it has been women who have been the main (unpaid) providers of care for the young, the old and for other dependent, vulnerable adults. In the 1980s, New Right governments began to talk about the state doing less and the family, together with the market and the voluntary sector, doing more. In respect of market provision, some have identified a paradigm shift in social provision from the late 1980s, resulting particularly in a shift to privatisation and decentralisation (of provision, although not always of financial control). Many countries are seeing the introduction of market principles (quasi-markets, to use the term of Le Grand and Bartlett)[4] into the public sector. Finally, voluntary sector provision has usually been omitted from larger comparative studies of welfare altogether. Major comparative studies, such as that of Esping Andersen,[5] have considered only state-provided welfare when they have sought to construct typologies of welfare regimes. As Kuhnle and Selle[6] have observed, if the voluntary sector is injected into Esping Andersen's typology, then any idea of a Scandinavian model disappears. Denmark, Norway and Sweden have had very different patterns of voluntary organisation.

Rather than seeing the story of the modern welfare state as a simple movement from individualism to collectivism and ever-increasing amounts of (benevolent) state intervention, it is more accurate to see European countries as having had mixed economies of welfare in which the state, the voluntary sector, employers, the family and the market have played different parts at different points in time.

The Theory of the Voluntary Sector

Voluntary sector provision has proved difficult to theorise and explain. Why have voluntary organisations arisen, and what has been their relationship with the state? There is a growing, mainly

American, literature which seeks to explain the existence of voluntary organisations and the role they play in social provision. Economists argue that they are the result of state or market failure. For example, Hansmann[7] has suggested that, where information asymmetries exist, contract failure occurs. Contract mechanisms may fail to provide consumers with the adequate means to police producers, and where consumers cannot evaluate services and need protection by providers, non-profit organisations will appear more trustworthy. Weisbrod[8] has stressed the extent to which the market or the state may fail to meet minority demands, which will then be met by voluntary organisations, but as the demand expands it will likely be met by the state. This kind of explanation tends to put the state, the market and the voluntary sector in separate boxes, such that the relationship between the state and the voluntary sector in particular becomes at best complementary and often conflictual. There is little room for the kind of conceptualisation of voluntary organisations as part and parcel of the fabric of the state that was the hallmark of nineteenth-century Britain and also seems to have characterised the Norwegian experience.[9]

Salamon's[10] theory of voluntary sector failure is more broadly in tune with the historical evidence. He has argued that voluntary organisations were perceived in most western countries as the first line of defence, but their weaknesses—insufficiency, particularism, paternalism and amateurism—rendered increasing co-operation with the state inevitable. The voluntary sector is so diverse and differs so greatly in its historical development between countries that it is highly unlikely that any single-discipline theory using a relatively small range of variables could be successfully applied to all cases. Thus while Hansmann's notion of contract failure fits the experience of US savings banks rather well (his chosen exemplar), it has little to offer the cases of social service provision in health, child welfare, education or housing in the USA, where different forms of voluntary/statutory co-operation seem to have prevailed.[11] Nor is it sufficient to explain why the provision of lifeboat services remains voluntary in Britain, but is a local government responsibility in Sweden, while the reverse is true of rural fire services.

What is important about Salamon's theory is therefore not so much the extent to which it fits the empirical evidence as the way in which it stresses the error of compartmentalising voluntary, statutory and market provision. Salomon prefers to look for the degree to which the boundaries between the sectors were in fact blurred. This is useful for the British case from the end of the nineteenth century, when the strict division between state provision, in the form of the poor law, and the market was significantly diminished, and when new forms of co-operation between the state and the voluntary sector, particularly in relation to government funding of voluntary organisations, became more common. But even this does not quite capture the complexity of the historical relationships, as Ware[12] has recognised. Late nineteenth-century charity leaders advocated close co-operation with the poor law while at the same time insisting on a separate sphere for charity. The point is that both the conceptualisation and the nature of the late nineteenth-century state were quite different from those of the late twentieth. Thus the meaning of a call for greater reliance on voluntary provision in the 1980s and 1990s will be different from a similar set of convictions in the 1870s and 1880s.

The Voluntary/Statutory Relationship[13]

In Britain at the end of the nineteenth century, it is likely that as much money passed through voluntary organisations as through the poor law. Certainly this was the case if the work of the medical charities is included. This surprised French observers at the time, who calculated that a large majority of British adults belonged to an average of between five or six voluntary organisations, which included: trades unions and friendly societies, both of which played a major role in securing for their members financial protection against sickness and unemployment; savings societies of various kinds; and literary and scientific institutes.[14] Charitable provision was exceedingly diverse and inevitably patchy. Nor was it just a top-down affair. Yeo[15] has shown how a late nineteenth-century British town (Reading) had thriving working-class voluntary organisations as well as middle-class philanthropy. Yeo, together with more recent commentators from the New Right, has suggested that the state's provision of (compulsory) social insurance in 1911 effectively destroyed existing mutual aid by trades unions and friendly societies. From the beginning of the twentieth century the balance in the mixed economy of welfare began to tilt in favour of the state.

It is important to understand how the 'idea' of charity has changed over time and how this has influenced notions of the proper relationship between the voluntary sector and the state. Arguably, such cultural variables are as important as more purely economic ones in determining the voluntary/statutory relationship. This relationship will be different for different countries, and my discussion here is confined to Britain.

At the turn of the century, debate about the proper role of charity was tied to discussion about citizenship. Some of the most influential leaders in the world of charity believed that charity amounted to a social principle. Charitable endeavour represented citizens united by moral purpose, voluntarily fulfilling their duty to those less fortunate than themselves. The idea was that better-off people would voluntarily perform their duty as citizens and help the poor to become fully participative members of society. The injunction to behave charitably thus amounted to a particular vision of an ethical society in which citizens motivated by altruism performed their duties towards one another voluntarily. The importance attached to participation in voluntary action as a necessary part of democratic society persisted; during the 1940s contrasts were drawn between the British state and Nazism in this respect.

Such ideals do not, of course, necessarily reflect what actually happened in practice. It was not for nothing that elderly people in the mid- and late-twentieth centuries remembered with bitterness having 'washed the charity' out of a garment. However, the way in which the place of charity was conceptualised means that it is mistaken to describe the nineteenth-century voluntary sector simply as something as big as or larger than statutory provision and as a wholly separate element from the state. Such a depiction consciously or unconsciously draws on the current conceptualisation of the voluntary sector as an alternative to the state and applies it to an earlier period.

It is more accurate to see voluntary organisations in the late nineteenth and early twentieth century as part of the way in which political leaders conceptualised the state. Jose Harris[16] has described the aim of Victorian governments as being 'to provide a framework of rules and guidelines designed to enable society very largely to run itself'. This did not amount to rank atomistic individualism: 'The corporate life of society was seen as expressed through voluntary associations and the local community, rather than through the persona of the state'. Nineteenth century Britain had effective central government institutions, but a small central bureaucracy (in stark contrast to the late twentieth century) and a strong desire to limit the activities of central government. Voluntary organisations may best be conceptualised as part of a range of 'buffer institutions'[17] that developed between the central state and the citizen and which were conceived of as being part of the fabric of the state. At the turn of the century, much state social provision was locally financed and administered. For example, the poor law was controlled by locally elected boards of guardians, and education by locally elected school boards. It was only from the beginning of the twentieth century that matters of social policy gradually became the stuff of 'high politics'. The fact that social provision was local made it easier for a measure of welfare pluralism to exist. During the 1980s and 1990s Conservative politicians in Britain have hankered after 'little battalions',[18] that is, social provision determined by community and neighbourhood. However, such an idea was arguably more feasible at the turn of the century when the central state left local territory relatively free from control.

At the turn of the century, leaders of major voluntary organisations and government had a common understanding of the role of charity and of the state in regard to the problem of poverty and pauperism. Both advocated co-operation between the statutory and voluntary sectors on similar tasks, while maintaining separate spheres of action. The voluntary principle was held to be extremely important because of the way in which charity was conceptualised as a social principle: there was no question, for example, of the state funding the voluntary sector.

It is possible to conceptualise this relationship as a form of 'partnership'. Indeed, government has talked continuously over time of partnership with the voluntary sector. The important point is that the meaning of the term has changed enormously. Finlayson[19] has used the concept of 'a moving frontier' to describe the relationship between the voluntary and the statutory sector. But the rather flabby term 'partnership' is probably more useful. At the turn of the century, the voluntary sector was seen as part and parcel of the body politic, working with the same principles as government in respect of social problems while carving out a separate sphere of action—what Beatrice and Sidney Webb[20] called the 'parallel bars' approach to the voluntary/statutory relationship. As government intervention increased with the provision of old-age pensions in 1908 and social insurance in 1911, and the role of the state grew bigger relative to that of the voluntary sector, so the nature of the partnership changed. Voluntary organisations began to take money from the state and to see themselves as *complementary* or *supplementary* providers of welfare. In 1934 Elizabeth Macadam wrote of the 'new philanthropy',[21] in which she called for closer co-operation between the state and voluntary organisations, by which she meant, not a partnership of equals, but rather voluntary organisations influencing and supplementing public services. In this formulation, voluntary organisations would no longer aim to be the first line of defence for social service as had been the case at the turn of the century.

This conceptualisation of partnership was strengthened after World War II with the setting up of the post-war welfare state. Sir William Beveridge, author of the blueprint for the post-war settlement, was himself a firm believer in voluntary action and harked back strongly to the turn-of-the-century insistence on the importance of the 'spirit of service'; the good society could only be built on people's sense of duty and willingness to serve.[22] Beveridge saw voluntary action as an important counterweight to the business motive and, like many others, as a fundamental ingredient of modern democracy. Voluntary organisations provided the opportunity for free association and participation, as well as variety and spontaneity. However, voluntary organisations were still perceived as supplementary, or at best complementary, to the state and the desirability of direct provision by the state was not questioned. During the period of the 'classic' welfare state (from 1945-1980), the relationship between economic growth and state social provision was believed to be positive, which resulted in a wholehearted commitment to state intervention to secure full employment, a redistributive social security system (although the actual extent of redistribution is debatable) that would enhance social consumption, and social services that were regarded as social investments.

The shift in thinking about the nature of the partnership between the voluntary and statutory sectors in the 1980s and 1990s has been profound. Government has consciously sought to promote the role of the voluntary sector as an *alternative* to the state, sometimes invoking the example of the late nineteenth century. However, the voluntary sector now relies heavily on paid as well as unpaid workers and on state financing, and operates in the context of a strongly centralised state. Late twentieth-century voluntary effort is no longer autonomous from that of the public sector. The 'tight/loose' organisation pioneered by private sector firms in the 1980s, involving the decentralisation of production and the centralisation of command, has been parallelled in the 'new public management' of the public sector. Since 1988 in Britain, and increasingly elsewhere, 'quasi-markets' have been introduced in all the social services—in health, housing, education and community care—with the voluntary sector becoming a major provider in housing and community care and the private sector a bigger provider in education, while health remains more of an internal market. But central government has set the parameters; the fiscal conditions have been set by the centre.

This makes the mixed economy of the late twentieth century very different from the mixed economy of the late nineteenth. Because post-war service-providing voluntary agencies have been funded primarily by government, their room for manoeuvre in the new situation is limited. While government has held out a larger role for them in social service provision, government is also in a position to say what it will contract with them to do. Voluntary organisations may be in the process of becoming alternative, rather than supplementary or complementary, providers of welfare, but in a situation in which the state determines the conditions of provision without taking responsibility. This form of welfare pluralism does not position voluntary agencies as mediating institutions, but tends rather to see them as instruments of the state, which raises difficult questions for agencies about both identity and function.

The Friendly Societies
and Adam-Smith Liberalism

David G. Green

IT is common to think of private charity as the primary alternative to the welfare state, whereas mutual aid associations
provided social security and even medical services for far more
people than did charities. When national insurance was first
enacted in Britain in 1911, over three-quarters of those covered
by the scheme (some nine million out of 12 million) were already
members of mutual aid associations. The nine million includes
unregistered societies. At the time, there were about 3.4 million
members of registered and unregistered trade unions.[1]

But the friendly societies were not merely organisations
providing welfare services. They, and the multiplicity of other
organisations that made up civil society, embodied the best
elements of Adam-Smith liberalism. It is necessary to speak of
Adam-Smith liberalism, and not merely of 'plain' liberalism,
because two quite different traditions of political philosophy have
come to be described by the term 'liberalism'. Perhaps the most
important difference between Adam-Smith liberalism and the
corrupted liberalism that emerged from the French Revolution
was that the former mistrusted the exercise of power and sought
to channel it to the service of the common good by confining it as
far as possible to the application of general laws. It was an ideal
of limited government which put its faith in co-operation in civil
society rather than in the political sphere. Its champions believed
that the interests of all would be best served, not within a social
order run by command from the top, but by private individuals
acting in mutual concert, seeking to improve their lives through
that combination of rivalry, co-operation and emulation that
typifies liberty at its best.

The corrupted liberalism of the nineteenth century (eventually
to evolve into the totalitarianism of the twentieth) believed in the
capacity of leaders to use government power to serve particular

purposes. Despite centuries of the abuse of discretionary power it did not mistrust power as such, but focused on *who* possessed it and *whose* interests were being served. But, as subsequent experiments were to demonstrate, all uses of discretionary power should be suspect, whether legitimised because they derived from 'the people' or not.

As Hayek[2] has shown, Adam-Smith liberals mistrusted both the older hierarchical view of society—which saw individuals as followers under the command of the monarch—as well as the newer corporatism. The liberalism of Adam Smith has often been called 'negative liberty' because of its mistrust of political power and as if it had no 'positive' dimension. But its suspicion of political power was the result of its faith in voluntary co-operation.

Individuals were not seen merely as people capable of playing a role under orders; they were looked upon as the imperfect but self-improving carriers of a moral compass. The national community to which each belonged was unified, not in the manner of an organisation run from the top, but by each member's support for the laws and institutions which comprise it. Leaders were not considered especially knowledgeable but as no less imperfect and capable of improvement than the citizens. Consequently, leaders were seen as replaceable. Because the power to govern was seen as necessary but open to abuse, it was to be exercised as far as possible through laws, not by arbitrary decision. And the task of government was to uphold the rules and the institutions indispensable to liberty and not to function as the head of an organisation with a purpose, save in war or national emergency.

The wish to limit political power was closely related to the liberal conception of morality. As countless liberal writers have argued, coercion could only be reduced if individuals were willing to restrain themselves from injuring others. Given human imperfection, some legal coercion was unavoidable but much judgement of right and wrong did not belong in the realm of coercion. The more moral responsibility that was assumed privately, the less the need for coercion. And the more people practised private responsibility the more their moral faculties developed so that the sphere of coercion could diminish still further. No less important, reserving moral debate for civil society meant that the moral order could change by a process of piecemeal adaptation. It was not 'morality as the crow flies', in Oakeshott's phrase.

This approach to morality placed a heavy burden of responsibility on private individuals, as parents and as participants in the organisations that make up their local communities. Each person's daily conduct was in some way a contribution to upholding or modifying the prevailing order. Every supportive frown or raised eyebrow as well as every complacent shrug of the shoulders made a difference. The value of a moral tradition that embraced both disapproval and toleration had been learnt from hard years of religious persecution.

Such were the main elements of the ideal of liberty upheld by writers such as Smith, Hume and Tocqueville. A free society for them should be made up of many organisations pursuing particular purposes but also based on liberal principles: a framework of rules, morals that were upheld but susceptible to gradual change, individuals guided by a sense of duty to others and aware that their personal contribution to upholding moral rules counted. And here lay the true significance of organisations like the friendly societies. They were examples of the best in this liberal tradition.

The Rise of Mutual Aid [3]

Membership of the friendly societies had grown steadily during the eighteenth century. The poor law return for 1803 estimated that there were 9,672 societies with 704,350 members in England and Wales alone.[4] By the time the British Government came to introduce compulsory social insurance under the 1911 National Insurance Act, there were 6.6 million members of registered friendly societies, quite apart from those not registered. The rate of growth of the friendly societies over the preceding thirty years had been accelerating.[5] In 1877, registered membership had been 2.75 million. Ten years later it was 3.6 million, increasing at an average of 85,000 a year. In 1897 membership had reached 4.8 million, having increased on average by 120,000 a year. And by 1910 the figure had reached 6.6 million, having increased at an annual average rate since 1897 of 140,000. Ironically they were at the height of their popularity when the Liberal government, which had fallen prey to statism, took the first steps towards unravelling liberal institutions like friendly societies with the introduction of compulsory national insurance in 1911.

Origins

At first the societies were local gatherings of men who knew each other and who met regularly to socialise over a drink. All members paid a regular contribution which gave them an agreed entitlement to benefit if they were too ill to work. The tradition among many early societies was that, if there was a surplus after the payment of benefits at the end of the year, it was divided up equally among members. The chief disadvantage of this system was that societies sometimes ran out of cash, and as a result federations began to develop from early in the nineteenth century. By the time of the Royal Commission on the Friendly Societies of 1874 there were 34 of them with over 1,000 members each. They developed and grew rapidly in response to industrial-isation, when workers felt a keen need for support in the new towns to which they had moved. In the areas experiencing the most rapid urbanisation, such as Lancashire and Yorkshire, where there was initially no sense of community, the friendly societies developed as fraternal alternatives to the tight-knit neighbourhoods more typical of rural areas. The largest society, the Manchester Unity of Oddfellows, grew rapidly after its foundation in 1814. In 1838 it had 90,000 members; by 1848, 249,000; and by 1876, just over half a million.

Among the reasons for their replacement of purely local clubs was the possibility of supporting members who had to travel in search of work. If a man lost his job, both the friendly societies and many trade unions provided 'travelling benefit', essentially assistance with the extra cost of searching for work. Members could journey throughout the UK in the hope of finding a new job and receive living expenses and mutual assistance while away from home. Proof of membership took the form of their equivalent of the plastic card and PIN—the quarterly password and the secret handshake.

Ethos

The ethos of the societies was formally taught in initiation ceremonies and lecture courses: a series of seven in the 600,000-strong Ancient Order of Foresters and four in the largest society, the Manchester Unity. The Foresters did not confine their advice to the conduct of society business:

> In your domestic relationships we look to find you, if a husband, affectionate and trustful; if a father, regardful of the moral and material

well-being of your children and dependants; as a son, dutiful and exemplary, and as a friend, steadfast and true.

In this manner the societies were a major force for self-improvement.

The societies sharply contrasted themselves with charities. Charity was one set of people helping others; mutual aid was putting money aside in a common fund and helping each other when the need arose. The benefits were rights:

> For certain benefits in sickness ... [we] subscribe to one fund. That fund is our Bank; and to draw therefrom is the independent and manly right of every Member, whenever the contingency for which the funds are subscribed may arise, as freely as if the fund was in the hand of their own banker, and they had but to issue a cheque for the amount. These are not BENEVOLENCES—they are rights.[6]

They often spoke of benefits as an entitlement and membership as creating solidarity. But their solidarity was that of individuals who had given something towards the common good. There was genuine reciprocity.

The Services

The paramount purpose of the friendly societies was independence. They provided all the services that enabled individuals to be self-supporting. If illness or injury struck, the friendly societies provided both a cash benefit and medical care, usually available through each society's own doctor, who was typically paid a capitation.

If the breadwinner died young, the society ensured that widow and orphans were provided for. Independence could also be threatened by old age, and again the societies provided support, though not in the form of a pension. Typically, members tried to keep working as long as possible with the fall-back of sick pay as age took its toll, with the friendly society nursing home as a last resort.

Thus, every member and his family was covered against the main dangers to independence: illness or injury, early death, old-age and temporary loss of job.

The success of the friendly societies was the result of the face-to-face involvement of members in the local branches which administered benefits. The members knew who was paying. It was not an anonymous 'them' but the members themselves.

Members felt they had a real stake in the organisation, and their sense of belonging not only discouraged manipulation of the system, but also created a genuine sense of fraternity. There was some fraud, but many members would not claim benefits at all, even when fully entitled. Moreover, the societies were not content merely to pay benefits. They arranged for sick members to be visited at least once a week, and every day if necessary.

The Societies and Participatory Democracy

In the branch, all Foresters met on equal terms:

> All meet there on terms of perfect equality ... No office is too high for the poorest to aspire to; no duty too humble for the richest to stoop to. Intelligence to govern, ability to exercise authority with becoming humility, yet with the requisite firmness, and personal demeanour to ensure respect, are all the qualifications for office required; and these are in the power of every Member to acquire.[7]

Each friendly society had its peculiarities but the Manchester Unity was representative. It was usual for lodges to try to find a competent permanent secretary and to keep him, but the other leading offices were rotated: the chairman, the vice-chairman and the immediate past chairman. All members were expected to seek to occupy these positions and for many manual workers the lodge offered opportunities to develop talents and skills for which their workplace provided no outlets. To overcome the disadvantages of rotation each chairman would appoint two supporters, a right and left supporter. They would sit on either side of him at meetings and offer advice as the meeting proceeded. Traditionally, the chairman chose an experienced right supporter, a member who was well informed about the rules and procedures. The left supporter was a friend. In this manner a high level of sharing of office was combined with efficient performance. This tradition of sharing office made the societies effective training academies for liberal democracy.

The Friendly Societies at the Turn of the Century

During the latter part of the nineteenth century new types of society began to develop as conditions changed. In particular, the desire for a balance between saving, on the one hand, and security in sickness and provision against death, on the other, led to the formation of deposit and Holloway societies. The

National Deposit Friendly Society was by far the largest of its type. Each member made a contribution which, after a deduction for management, went partly to a common fund for sick pay and partly to a personal account which accumulated at interest. Members could choose the size of their contribution so long as it was no less than 2s per month and no more than 20s. This contribution then determined the benefit: the daily rate of sick benefit was the same as the monthly rate of contribution. In addition, each member was urged on joining to make an initial deposit to their personal account. Sick pay was drawn partly from the common fund and partly from the member's personal account in a proportion which varied with age at joining. It was payable until the member's personal account was exhausted, which meant that a person who did not experience much illness would accumulate a large surplus by retirement age.

Conclusions

The friendly societies were not just benefit societies. They treated people as if they had a moral dimension to their character as well as a material one. They appealed to the best in people, and enabled them to face the challenges of leadership and self-organisation. When national insurance was introduced it attended only to the material dimension, and in separating the cash benefits from the moral and educational role of the societies destroyed their essence.

The welfare state that replaced mutual aid was built on a complex of ideas standing in opposition to older doctrines of reciprocal obligation evolved by the friendly societies. There were two main intellectual departures. First political parties fighting the class-war attempted to equalise people. Their efforts had a corrupting effect on the democratic process, turning it into a battleground for private advantage rather than a process of making laws for the common good. Second, entitlement was justified by the pretence of insurance. Germany began social insurance in the 1880s, but it was never true insurance. Nevertheless, in countries that introduced the insurance principle, it awakened expectations of rights that had not been earned.

In many European countries, the systems that emerged under the influence of these ideas relied heavily on governments giving workers rights by imposing obligations on employers. In addition, there were often restrictions on the employer's ability to hire and fire, and administrative systems of wage fixing. It was taken for granted that there was reasonably stable, full-time employment and that employers were large enough to have legal requirements imposed on them by governments. Today these assumptions can not be made. Most people work for small employers. There are few 'jobs for life'. There is much more part-time work, more self-employment and more people work on fixed-term contracts.

The earlier approach of the friendly societies was based, not on imposing obligations on employers, but on the importance of equipping individuals to cope with the uncertainty of global competition. Most of us will have several jobs during our working lives and we need the strength and resources to overcome difficulties when between jobs or unable to work. This tradition of reciprocal obligation treated people as capable of exercising responsibility. It sought to increase their human capital and, by fostering civil society, to increase their social capital so that no one stood alone.

Private Provision and Public Welfare: Health Insurance Between the Wars

Noel Whiteside

Introduction

RECENT trends in social policy reform have emphasised the advantages of privatising welfare, of separating service purchase from service provision through the creation of internal markets in health and social services. The aim has been to stimulate efficiency, to secure better value for money and to offer greater choice to consumers by utilising a variety of private agencies in the administration of public policies. Following the General Election of May 1997, the Labour government stressed the significance of reinforcing partnerships between public and private sectors to enable the transfer of social dependents from welfare to work, to foster the development of new systems of social protection and to help in overcoming problems of growing social exclusion. In abandoning the centralised, bureaucratic state structures created in the 1940s, we may possibly return to the welfare systems of an earlier age. For, under the National Health Insurance (NHI) scheme, which administered both social security benefits and basic health care to workers between 1912 and 1948, private 'approved societies' competed for members, offering statutory medical treatments and cash benefits in return for a fixed tri-partite contribution, operating under the supervision of the Ministry of Health.

This paper explores how these agencies combined public provision with incentives to private protection, revealing how public and private sectors worked together in an effort to extend medical care and sickness benefits in these years. It evaluates the performance of both mutual and commercial agencies involved in state welfare. Did competition secure an efficient

Research for this paper was funded by the ESRC under the Whitehall Programme. The author would like to thank Peter Hennock, Christian Toft and David Green for comments on earlier drafts.

allocation of resources? Did public subsidy help foster—or drive out—personal thrift and voluntary protection? What kinds of choice were available to consumers ? And, finally, if quasi-market systems like this one do display the advantages their advocates claim, why was the scheme abolished after the Second World War? In re-examining the debates of the 1940s in the political climate of the 1990s, we are presented with the case against those pro-market arguments which gained extensive credibility in the years of the Thatcher and Major governments.

However, we cannot argue that circumstances in inter-war Britain were the same as they are today. The responsibilities of government for pre-war welfare remained essentially residual. By and large, those who could afford to pay were required to pay, a situation which only changed with the advent of the mixed economy and universalism in state welfare during the later 1940s. Before the war, separate statutory social insurance schemes—providing benefits for the unemployed, the sick and (from 1925) the elderly, widows and orphans—were confined to the working class. Publicly funded health services, run by local authorities, operated alongside the NHI scheme; these provided maternity and infant welfare clinics, school medical services, treatments for venereal disease and tuberculosis, institutional care for a range of infectious diseases and mental problems and some domiciliary nursing services. During the 1930s, when poor law infirmaries (which had provided for the destitute sick) were transferred to local authorities, publicly funded provision tended to expand in more prosperous areas of the country. Even so, throughout this period, middle-class consumers paid their own doctors' bills and were excluded from statutory social insurance. Yet the inter-war era, characterised by high unemployment and strict constraints on public expenditure, bears more than a passing resemblance to our own. Then, as now, industrial recession increased the numbers dependent on the public purse. This stimulated policies designed to reduce state liabilities by restricting access to state benefits,[1] limiting Exchequer subsidies, fostering voluntary and charitable agencies and promoting private provision of welfare. Here, administrative efficiency and cost effectiveness were at a premium. Without arguing that history repeats itself, this chapter suggests that similar policy perspectives in the two periods generated welfare systems which displayed similar strengths and weaknesses. These similarities will be explored below.

In historical terms, much more attention has been dedicated to the establishment of National Health Insurance (NHI) in 1911 than to its subsequent operation, although the relationship between government, approved societies and the medical profession has received detailed attention.[2] In general, historians have followed the criticisms presented in the 1942 Beveridge Report when evaluating the system's performance and explaining its demise.[3] Consequently, NHI is primarily criticised for inequity. Different societies offered different degrees of protection for the same contribution; the best services were provided for those who needed them least, because the richer societies tended to recruit healthy and to reject unhealthy applicants. These distortions are explained by the involvement of commercial agencies (industrial insurance companies) as approved societies, which allowed the promotion of private profit to take precedence over the protection of public welfare.[4] As a result, unlike the German health insurance scheme (which served as a precedent but which never involved commercial interests), the British scheme failed to thrive. While not denying that the system generated inequalities—as any market will—this account will query such explanations, suggesting instead that comparative failure was due less to the activities of insurance companies than to tight central regulation and the vulnerability of the scheme's finances to raids by the Treasury. The appearance of market competition and agency independence was illusory. Hence an analysis of this system—of how NHI really worked—is significant for any understanding of more recent social policy developments; private agencies involved in welfare provision are as vulnerable to funding changes and central direction as any public equivalent.

National Health Insurance:
Approved Society Autonomy and Central Control

To evaluate this form of welfare, its structure and operation require explanation. The National Health Insurance scheme, the brainchild of Lloyd George, lasted from 1912 until 1948, combining what we would now classify as social security benefits and a rudimentary health service. It offered basic GP care and sickness benefits in return for a tri-partite contribution, covering all workers earning less than a specified minimum annual income—but not their families and dependants. In addition to those included by statute, the scheme was open to voluntary contributors: about 640,000 were included by 1936.[5] The scheme was administered by centrally registered 'approved' societies (friendly societies, industrial insurance companies and a few trade unions) which administered benefits, paid the 'panel' doctors and dispensaries through local insurance committees and generally managed the day-to-day running of the scheme. Approved societies were non-profit making; they were originally designed to promote consumer participation and to offer choice. While all societies were obliged to provide the statutory minimum, the larger, richer societies could attract new recruits by using profits made under the scheme to fund 'additional' benefits (mostly ophthalmic and dental care, specialist services or extra cash payments) for their members. This element of competition promoted careful administration to safeguard society funds; yet societies tended to help claimants because callous treatment could alienate prospective members. Additional benefits were important to attract new recruits; societies sought, with official endorsement, to encourage their members to purchase private policies to 'top up' the public one and it was through the extension of this private business that the societies (notably the industrial insurance companies) made their profits. The number of working people covered by the scheme expanded from around 11.5 million in 1912 to 20.264 million in 1938 (out of a total population of 47.5 million)[6]—an expansion explained by population growth, by raising of the ceiling of minimum annual earnings to £250 in 1920 and by the rising numbers of women covered by the scheme (from 3.68 million in 1912 to 6.11 million in 1938).[7]

Despite appearances to the contrary, central control over society activities was strong. All society monies accruing under the scheme ended up in the coffers of the Ministry of Health. Employers purchased stamps from the GPO, stuck them each week in the NHI book of each employee (deducting the worker's contribution from wages). The book was returned to the worker's chosen approved society, which returned it to the ministry as proof of income—which, in turn, credited the society's internal account. Actual cash was only paid over on receipt of six-monthly audited accounts; societies were reimbursed retrospectively and any 'improper' expenditure (which did not conform to central regulations or society rules) was not repaid. Every five years, the Government Actuary—who was charged with securing the financial viability of each individual society—used these audited accounts to predict future profitability. His valuations determined the amount of future profit to be used to fund additional benefits, the amount to be held centrally in contingency funds, the amount to be dedicated to investments—both by the society itself and central government acting on its behalf. Three points should be noted. First—contrary to historical assumption—the system made it quite impossible for NHI profits to be transferred to the pockets of society officials or to shareholders or anyone else. Second, it was easy for the ministry to tighten regulations governing access to benefit unilaterally. As the Exchequer contribution was only paid on reimbursement of expenditure, inter-war governments had a built-in incentive to reduce successful claims as far as possible. Third, by the early 1940s, large sums had accrued to society accounts held within Whitehall as contingency funds; the interest on these was used to offset the Exchequer contribution—to the tune of £7 million out of £9 million per year.[8] In short, NHI came to cost the middle-class taxpayer very little indeed.[9]

The inter-war depression reinforced central authority over society activity. Recession reduced contributory income, raised the incidence of claims and generated cuts in public subsidy. Simultaneously, growing political pressure sought to extend both the unemployment and health benefit rights of those losing work. Amending legislation repeatedly extended and redefined the rights of the unemployed to statutory benefits, including health benefits, at the expense of approved societies.[10] In 1939 the unemployed could still claim one to two years' free insurance; ten-year members were allowed to sustain NHI cover indefinitely, on an annual rolling basis.[11] At the same time, as obligations increased, society income from the Exchequer was repeatedly reduced—once in 1922 (following the Geddes committee report) and twice in 1925 (following the introduction of contributory pensions[12] and the Economy Act[13]). Years later, this still provoked anger, particularly among poorer societies, over monies 'filched by the Chancellor'.[14] These cuts were never restored. The 1932 crisis, as unemployment rates peaked and the run on gold reserves provoked another round of public expenditure cuts, was met by reducing women's benefit rights and removing cover from some unemployed. A central fund was established to bail out societies in trouble, financed by collective contributory income.[15] Constant cuts and rising liabilities took their toll on small, local societies—some of which collapsed under the strain.[16] The effects of prolonged recession undermined the principles of social insurance just as surely in the inter-war period as in recent years. Society profits were transformed into savings for the Treasury, not better benefits for the public, as the scheme's founders had originally intended.

This outline of the financial structure and development of health insurance demonstrates how the system extended social protection at the price of undermining society autonomy—a process reinforced by recession. 'Our secretaries are simply being converted into State officials ...' the Manchester Unity of Oddfellows representative complained in March 1914.

> It is said that the funds have been administered by self-governing societies, but then we know as a matter of fact that they are not self-governing.[17]

Time made this position worse. Constant changes in regulations governing the rights of the unemployed with varying contributory status—women claimants, voluntary contributors or members aged over 65—all increased the authority of those few Whitehall officials who governed the scheme while mystifying society secretaries and their members. Ministry officials safeguarded society solvency by policing claims and doctors' certification procedures. In a manner strongly reminiscent of recent reassessments of claimants to incapacity benefits, numbers of centrally appointed regional medical officers supplemented the work of society sickness visitors, inspecting long-term claimants with a view to finding them fit for work.[18] These inspections can be understood as the health insurance equivalent of the better known local employment committees, which interrogated claimants to unemployment benefit to ascertain whether they had been 'genuinely seeking work'.[19]

In spite of these problems, societies performed efficiently, evidently better than the employment exchanges charged with the running of the centralised unemployment insurance scheme. 'Sound' (meaning efficient) administration could secure profits to fund additional benefits and attract members. In 1922-4, evidently impressed by their performance, two major enquiries into state social insurance (covering health, unemployment and the proposed contributory pensions scheme) investigated how administration of all state benefits might be unified under the approved societies.[20] This promised to remove duplicate administrative structures and the expense of shuffling marginal claimants between different agencies as each scheme sought to minimise its liabilities. Thanks to resistance from the Ministry of Labour and the trade unions, the initiative collapsed. When the question of unification was re-examined by the Beveridge Committee in 1942, the response to problems of administrative duplication went the other way—in spite of extensive evidence on the superior administrative performance of the approved societies in collecting contributions, processing claims and the policing of possible fraud.

The benefits of efficient administration were, however, offset by other questions of cost.[21] In 1913-14, central audit inspected the books of nearly 19,000 separate units. Between 1912 and 1924, the number of societies involved in NHI fell from 2,208 to 1,194—falling again to 859 by 1935—but, taking branches still liable for separate audit into account, this still involved central regulation of 6,339 agencies, the largest of which had 2.4 million members and the smallest 34.[22] Transactions between member and society as well as society and central authority, between doctor and patient, between doctor and local insurance committee, all translated into administrative expense and higher costs—particularly in the case of the industrial insurance companies which employed an army of agents. As central government only provided a nominal subsidy towards staffing, the system survived on unpaid—or grossly underpaid—labour.[23] Beveridge calculated that the administration of NHI absorbed 17 per cent of contributory income, far more than the unemployment scheme, without including additional expenses incurred by audit and actuarial work, nor by the duplication of capital equipment and buildings. The attractions of using private agencies for welfare delivery lie largely in the 'efficiency savings' they promise on staff costs. However, this is a question of swings and roundabouts. What the taxpayer saves on service delivery is spent on regulation and audit. Further, the contributor pays for the costs of competition—in duplicated capital equipment, buildings and staffing. Hardly surprising, therefore, that Beveridge stressed the economies of scale to be found in a centralised, state-run service.

Approved Society Performance: Consumers, Competition and Choice

The administrative advantages offered by approved societies— their association with efficient management and the promotion of voluntary thrift—were closely bound up with the issue of competition. Originally, NHI was designed to promote democratic self-government in benefit administration; additional medical treatments would reflect membership demand as competition for members would guarantee responsiveness to members' needs. However, popular participation in the governance of societies was never strong; more commercially oriented companies—the industrial insurance companies and centralised friendly societies— expanded slightly during this period at the expense of friendly societies with branches and trade unions, which embodied those traditions of mutuality that Lloyd George had wanted to promote.

Attempts to extend mutuality failed from the outset. When the Liverpool Victoria collecting society, with three million members nationwide (one million in London), advertised its first AGM in 1913 only 20 people turned up. 'That shows to my mind' their representative informed a departmental committee 'that people are only concerned as to getting their benefits and that though the mutual idea is recognised in theory, it does not work out in practice'.[24] Friendly societies expected members to attend branch meetings to deliver and collect their cards, staying to run society business. By the Second World War this tradition was fading,[25] probably because central regulation throttled the possibility of popular participation. Early efforts by members of the Tunbridge Wells Equitable Approved Society (TWEAS) to influence society policy, for example, were over-ruled by central authority as contrary to regulations.[26] Membership attendance at their AGM remained small, 70 out of 28,000 members attending in 1913 (rising to 250 of 63,000 members in 1930) and those present were mostly branch officials.[27] Inspection of *The Equitable* (the society's magazine) reveals a different picture. The journal is replete with notices of collective jollity: carnival dances, annual dinners and branch outings, bank holiday trips, seaside visits, juvenile tea entertainments and juvenile outings, demonstrating how a healthy medium-sized friendly society in a prosperous part of the country responded to the social requirements of its membership and secured its next generation of recruits.[28] Operating in an area of low unemployment and having few members in dangerous trades, this society subsidised 'extra-curricular' activities through high returns on those investments under its control. Its profitability secured immunity to official pressures to use sickness visitors or to police its panel doctors, unlike poorer societies (the National Union of Foundry Workers for example) whose profits were far less secure. For societies in surplus, however, interest payments from investments under their control could subsidise additional activities, or offset disallowed reimbursement, or finance social events.[29]

In the drive to secure members, commercial acumen and central business organisation prospered at the expense of more democratic organisation. Among trade-union approved societies, lack of commercial expertise, poor recruitment from the outset[30] and the advent of high unemployment in coal mining, ironfounding, engineering and shipbuilding all generated financial difficulties. As the inter-war recession deepened, so workers with chronic conditions became 'residualised' as long-term claimants on disability benefits, of whom trade union societies recruiting in heavy industry had more than their share. Hence trade union societies (with the exception of the London Compositors) offered fewer additional benefits than others and were the most vociferous advocates of pooling profits to fund general provision. Following the debacle of the 1926 General Strike, the National Association of Trade Union Approved Societies (NATUAS) initiated a drive to repair union organisation through the extension of approved society membership (similar to the initiatives being discussed within the TUC today); this, unable to match the services and care of more prosperous societies, ultimately gained little ground.[31]

In contrast, the industrial insurance companies' public and private business expanded in this period. Voluntary insurance grew on an unprecedented scale, particularly life insurance. By 1939, 2.25 private policies existed for every UK citizen; premium income on these policies—at £74 million p.a.—was more than the total contributions of employers and employed to state schemes for health, unemployment and pensions combined.[32] Four out of five private policies were held by 14 major companies (the rest being shared between 146 collecting societies).[33] Of these companies, the Prudential was easily the largest, running four approved societies with a membership of over 4.3 million and holding 29 million private policies.[34]

The Beveridge Report was highly critical of enormous profits from lapsed policies, the amounts paid to shareholders and the expenses incurred by using insurance agents—arguing strongly (endorsing the TUC view) that commercial interests should not be associated with the administration of state social welfare.[35] However, the personal attention provided by agents was popular, particularly among sectors of the working population repudiated by friendly societies and trade unions—including many women workers. The individual attention and help afforded by the company agent was preferred to the impersonal reception claimants received at the employment exchanges. Competition fostered responsiveness; as approved society profits could only be spent on benefits, NHI activities could be used as a loss leader to attract private business.

'[I]t has been frequently suggested to us', a departmental committee reported in 1914:

> that the agent of industrial insurance societies is urged to an attitude of undue leniency with those with whom it is necessary he should live on amicable terms, if he is successfully to carry out his ordinary business.[36]

Friendly societies complained that commercial companies gave sickness benefits to all comers; societies who policed their members lost them.[37] In similar vein, the panel doctors were constantly accused, again by mainstream friendly societies, of signing certificates on demand, to keep registered patients (and the *per capita* fee). 'We never saw toothache, earache and headache [on a doctor's certificate] until the National Insurance Act commenced operations', grumbled the Manchester Unity of Oddfellows.[38] The advent of the state scheme provoked a reconstruction of sickness as evidence of an inability to work. Accusations of 'lax certification' plagued the NHI scheme throughout the inter-war years, re-emerging in evidence to the Beveridge Committee.[39] One of the arguments for setting up a state-run health service was that, as government employees, GPs would be liable to stricter official controls.

Competition also produced less desirable consequences. In selecting their clientele, all approved societies preferred the young, the healthy, the regularly employed. Successful societies were able to offer better benefits to a predominantly healthy membership while poorer ones tended to have higher rates of claim, low (or no) profits and therefore few additional benefits. The widely acknowledged problem of adverse selection was not, however, the product of commercialism. Traditionally, friendly societies had exacted higher entrance fees from older entrants and required all new members to undergo a medical examination.

Very few women gained membership. They were usually accom-
modated in separate branches, reflecting their lower earning
capacity and worse sickness experience which could otherwise
threaten society solvency. Working class mutuality was successful when it was selective. In contrast, the industrial insurance
companies admitted all comers. 'We have taken in the halt, the
maim and the blind', the Prudential boasted to the Beveridge
Committee 'and we have never asked for a medical certificate in
respect of any person ...'[40] By contrast, the Tunbridge Wells
Equitable rejected candidates in poor health and reviewed all
with a history of tuberculosis in the family on a case by case
basis.[41] That competition stimulated segregation and thus,
indirectly, skewed the distribution of medical care, there can be
little doubt. However, such practices developed from friendly
society convention; they were neither the product of commercial-
isation nor the consequence of state control.

Internal markets are supposed to stimulate competition; the
NHI scheme was competitive, but only within limits. When the
scheme first started, competition was initially fierce; societies
recruited through advertisements in newspapers, railway
stations, bus depots, working men's clubs. However, after a
period of frenetic activity, competitive activity waned, for several
reasons. First, member transfers were time consuming and
expensive; the TWEAS recorded the loss of 250 members and the
gain of 1,000 in 1914; each transaction required medical
certification, the calculation of transfer credits and the alteration
of accounts at local and central level.[42] Such complications
meant that societies came to dislike transfers, especially as most
'transferees' were workers in poor health trying to join a society
that might offer them better benefits. Second, societies federated
into master associations for political purposes: NATUAS was
founded in 1913, as was the Association of Approved Societies
and the National Federation of Employers' Approved Societies,
among others. These formed internal cartels, controlling poach-
ing and limiting competition.[43] Third, in time, members became
tied to their societies. After 1918, transferees lost their rights to
additional benefits for five years; most additional benefits and
private policies rewarded long-term members.

Additional benefits formed the chief attraction for new recruits;
by 1939, 85.5 per cent of approved society members could claim
some additional benefits,[44] although this figure had dipped

considerably during the slump. These benefits took the form of cash payments to cover medical costs, providing a real element of consumer choice—whether to join the Royal Liver (offering half-cost up to a maximum £5 on medical appliances) or the Hearts of Oak (offering full-cost up to £1 and half-cost thereafter),[45] for example. Full-cost cover for dentistry was rarely offered, as this would stimulate unnecessary treatments; the benefit tended to be undersubscribed, partly because dentistry was unpleasant, partly because the member still paid part of the bill. Although the form and nature of additional benefits varied widely, there is little evidence that new entrants shopped around for the society best suited to their needs. Most joined the society neighbours, friends or parents knew. Small local societies —offering fewer additional benefits than the larger, more commercial alternatives—survived into the 1940s, thanks to this parochialism.

Securing Reform and Abolishing the Market: Debates of the 1940s

Arguments voiced against the approved society system in the 1940s were audible in the 1920s. NHI medical services remained independent of local authority health services; they were not subject to the medical officer of health's control, and this disrupted local planning. In 1925 a Royal Commission on National Health Insurance had demanded the separation of medical services from the insurance system, to allow these to be publicly planned and funded, a recommendation endorsed by both the National Conference of Friendly Societies and the NATUAS.[46] Ministry of Health officials, the BMA, the local medical officers of health were all committed to regional organisation and rationalisation for local health services.[47] The transfer of poor law medical services to local authorities in 1929 offered the opportunity to further this aim. Dental services, rheumatic treatments and other forms of specialist care straddled the divide between public health and NHI, complicating access, transaction costs and distribution.[48] Clear internal demarcation lines emerged within the Ministry of Health between those who favoured the extension of health services through NHI (the controller, the BMA and the voluntary hospitals) and those who argued for public provision (the chief medical officer, the school medical services, the general hospitals, the local medical officers of health).

Various compromises were proposed. A committee on Scottish health services advocated the extension and rationalisation of local authority provision 'to avoid the unnecessary duplication of expensive buildings and equipment and to secure the maximum use of highly specialised skills', combining this with an extension of GP cover under NHI.[49] A Political and Economic Planning (PEP) report advocated similar reforms, but retained dental and specialist services under NHI (the Scottish report wanted these transferred to local authorities).[50] During the early 1930s, the Labour-led London County Council demonstrated the advantages of a purely public service by rationalising hospital care, providing common staffing standards, funding back-up laboratories and generating the infrastructure of what emerged as a mini NHS before the war.[51] This experiment provided a blueprint for Labour's post-war health policy, operating under the direct gaze of Westminster and Whitehall.

On the social security side, the existence of approved societies blocked Beveridge's plans to unify social insurance, his aim since the early 1920s.[52] In this area, his mind was already made up. During 1941, he undertook an extensive investigation into the private profits of industrial insurance companies and into the administrative costs of running separate schemes of state social insurance, with the view to using this material to justify the plan he had already established in his mind.[53] The approved societies had, in his eyes, a number of disadvantages. Rising labour mobility did not fit well with localised health insurance and the provision of separate classifications for causes of job-loss generated extensive, time-wasting inter-departmental and inter-agency disputes (not just between Ministry of Labour and Ministry of Health, but also between industrial insurance companies, trade unions and friendly societies over the handling of borderline cases of workmen's compensation).[54] The extension and unification of social insurance offered attractive economies of scale.[55] Further, all societies had idiosyncratic procedures and there was no independent guidance or advice for new entrants about which to select. Finally, and most famously, the system generated unequal returns for equal contributions. An unified state-run system offered simplification, social justice and substantial savings in administrative costs: 'Collecting money voluntarily is, of course, expensive', Beveridge informed the Prudential's representatives on 16 June 1942, 'particularly if you do it by collectors. Collecting it compulsorily is cheap'.[56] The abolition of the approved society system was supported by the TUC, a variety of left-of-centre pressure groups, local government organisations, the Shipping Federation and—surprisingly—the Association of Approved Societies.[57]

Not that these arguments proved conclusive. The friendly societies (through the National Confederation of Friendly Societies, with eight million members) fought right to the drafting of the 1946 National Insurance Bill to be incorporated as administrative agencies;[58] Beveridge tabled an unsuccessful amendment to this effect when the bill came before the House of Lords.[59] During the 1945 election, 199 Labour candidates pledged themselves to support friendly and trade union societies, in the name of democratic socialism.[60] In debates in the Commons, Labour and Conservative MPs argued fiercely for the retention of the old system. 'I plead for human administration, such as was given personally by the industrial agent in the past', one Labour MP said, 'a type of service in which, when sickness came, the people found that they had someone in the agent who was friendly and who helped or advised them or, when death came, the widow found there was someone who took the emotional load off her'.[61] Beveridge's distaste for the commercial sector was not universally shared by those on the political left.

The justifications used by the government to reject such pleading were rooted in the objectives of administrative rationalisation and the promotion of uniform treatment. In the post-war era, labour-intensive systems of benefit administration could not be justified when labour shortages were so critical. Under Labour's 1946 National Insurance Act, one office would deal with all hardship, guaranteeing equity of treatment and minimising the numbers of officials required to deal with claims[62] (implicitly allowing the maximum numbers to return to manufacturing production). The post-war debates have to be set in their political and economic environment, in which economies of scale and overall administrative cost reductions appeared alongside questions of equity and social justice in vindicating a new approach.

> The present arrangement, which allows 437 local units to give benefits in Liverpool, 248 in Bolton, 324 in Brighton and 241 in Norwich is uneconomic. In Dundee, 61 out of 219 units had only one member apiece and 54 had only 2-9 members in 1942. A carefully planned state machinery would effect a saving in expense.[63]

Support for centralised administration was also reflected in the new National Health Service, in the rationalisation of local government and in the creation of new civil service hierarchies.[64] Post-war reform of social security conformed to common principles underpinning the extension of public services, valuing uniformity and equity over variety, competition and choice— professionalism over democratic controls (or consumer power). These systems were put in place in a changed economic environment, now concerned to minimise both public and private costs. Economic policy in the inter-war years—as today—had been obsessively concerned with levels of *public* expenditure, assuming private administrative costs to be contained by commercial pressures. Beveridge was not interested in this private/public distinction and focused on overall costs of specific types of service delivery: here, the public regulation of private markets emerged as a more expensive option. In a post-war era more receptive to Keynesian argument and supportive of state intervention, this analysis was persuasive. As government has been moved to 'roll back the state' in recent years, so perspectives have changed; we have returned to the economic assumptions of earlier years and the welfare strategies that characterise them.

Conclusions

It remains to assess the advantages and disadvantages of this public/private partnership: its efficiency, its promotion of private thrift to supplement public provision and its effects on the distribution of welfare. A number of positive features emerge. First, the scheme proved to be more responsive to its clientele than the system that succeeded it. The opposition of Labour MPs to the abolition of NHI sprang not simply from a desire to protect traditions of mutuality, but also, surprisingly, indicated support for industrial insurance companies whose agents provided the personal advice unobtainable from centralised bureaucracies of later years. This was important in those areas and to those people that the early friendly societies had left comparatively untouched—notably women workers. Second, the scheme was administratively efficient; approved societies were better at collecting industrial contributions, maintaining records and distributing benefits than the state-run employment exchanges. Third, the statistics show that private social protection was extended under state sponsorship; friendly society policies were sustained, commercial life insurance spread. While Beveridge rightly condemned commercial profits derived from lapsed policies, these lapses were in part due to the sudden rise in unemployment caused by the slump in the 1930s, a catastrophe whose consequences for household economies cannot solely be laid at the industrial insurance companies' door. If the object of state welfare is to extend personal responsibility for social protection, then NHI was a success. In addition, the traditions of conviviality and community activity were sustained, even extended, by the involvement of parent friendly societies under the NHI scheme.

The merits of the scheme, however, should not be exaggerated. We cannot conclude that NHI could (and should) have been retained as an alternative to a National Health Service. Unlike German health insurance, the British scheme did not expand and thrive as Lloyd George had intended. Statutory coverage remained restricted to contributors alone (and not to their families); although additional benefits became relatively wide-spread, the scope of statutory medical treatments was never extended. Hence the introduction of the NHS revealed the poor health experienced by married women who had been excluded from the scheme. This failure of NHI, however, was not the consequence of some sort of triumph of private interest over the public good. On the contrary, it was due to tight state regulation and the Treasury's decision to convert society profits into public expenditure savings rather than let them be used for better medical care or wider coverage. This is not to argue that an unregulated system would have performed better. On the contrary, extensions of statutory protection to unemployed people (whose contributions had lapsed) helped some of the poorest and most vulnerable; without state action, their access to medical care and sickness benefits would have disappeared. The problem was not state regulation *per se*, but the highly conservative nature of political priorities. In this example of a public/private partnership, the societies were badly betrayed.

To the planners of the 1940s, NHI appeared archaic; its duplication of administrative staffs and buildings, its high running costs and its uneven provision of treatment reflected deep-rooted inefficiencies. The skewed distribution of better services to those who needed them least proved a damning indictment. In an age that prioritised equity, the abolition of NHI offered the opportunity to secure economies of scale and to plan resources according to need. In the 1940s access to health care became a right for all. In the 1980s and 1990s we have observed the pendulum swinging the other way. Equity is no longer a priority; efficiency is no longer understood as a natural consequence of planning, but as a product of market systems, of competitive allocative mechanisms. We appear to be going round in circles. The only way to break the spiral is to recognise that the division between state and market is nebulous. All markets are publicly regulated and operate in accordance with an implicit set of social conventions. Public regulation of private provision does not suddenly allow welfare to be distributed according to impartial rules or some hidden hand. On the contrary, as this historical case study illustrates, it offers an alternative system of public administration, as vulnerable to central direction as any publicly-owned counterpart, with its own set of strengths and weaknesses.

Political Thought and the Welfare State 1870-1940: An Intellectual Framework for British Social Policy

Jose Harris

A Change of Outlook

LEGISLATION after the Second World War created in Britain one of the most uniform, centralised, bureaucratic and 'public' welfare systems in Europe, and indeed in the modern world. Yet a social analyst of a hundred years ago would have observed and predicted the exact opposite: that the provision of social welfare in Britain was and would continue to be highly localised, amateur, voluntaristic and intimate in scale by comparison with the more coercive and *étatist* schemes of her continental neighbours (in particular imperial Germany). Numerous social policy inquiries of the 1880s, 1890s and 1900s uncovered a vast, ramshackle mass of voluntary, self-governing, local, parochial and philanthropic provision that was attempting in a myriad of different ways to assist, elevate, reform or coerce the poor and other persons in need. The annual income and expenditure of registered and unregistered charities, friendly societies, collecting societies, benefit-paying trade unions and other benevolent and self-help institutions vastly exceeded the annual budget of the poor law—which in turn vastly exceeded the expenditure on social welfare of central government until just before the First World War.[1] However imperfectly geared to meeting the needs of its clients, this mass of voluntary and local

This chapter first appeared as an article in *Past and Present*, Vol. 135, May 1992, pp. 116-41 and is reproduced here by permission. It forms part of a larger project on the intellectual history of the welfare state, supported by the British Academy and the Nuffield Foundation.

institutions was clearly an integral part of the social structure and civic culture of the country. It expressed and reinforced the distribution of power and resources, class and patronage relationships, behavioural norms and community identity. It was also closely interwoven with the system of natural and personal liberty by which many British people believed that their lives were differentiated from those of the rest of the world.

The structural transformation of welfare provision that oc-curred in Britain between the 1870s and the 1940s was therefore of central importance, not simply in the history of social policy, but in the wider history of politics, government, social structure and national culture. How did it come about that Victorian social welfare provision—largely purveyed through face-to-face relation-ships within the medium of civil society—evolved into the most 'rational' and bureaucratic of modern welfare states? That there were many practical, material and functional pressures in the direction of bureaucratic centralisation is undeniable. Through-out the period the increasing scale of economic organisation, the inadequate tax-base of local government, the erosion of paternal-ist community structures, the impact of demographic change and the inescapably 'national' character of certain key social prob-lems (especially unemployment) all combined to shift the British welfare system in the direction of centralised financing and control, without anyone specifically willing that this should come about. To a certain extent the free market itself facilitated and even compelled state intervention by subverting many of the traditional local and voluntary relationships on which the so-called 'minimal state' relied. But material pressures alone are not wholly adequate as a medium of explanation, since such pressures have existed in all advanced industrial countries —many of which have retained, or even moved towards, a much more localised, pluralistic and self-governing element in the management of modern welfare.[2] It seems reasonable, therefore, to look more closely at the role of ideas and ideology—at the legitimising framework of social thought that either conditioned or expressed the changing pattern of British social policy between 1870 and the Second World War. No suggestion is intended here that social and political theories were the sole or major factor in bringing about structural change; simply the claim that ideas were one among many variables, that they were an important part of the wider culture of social reform, and that at the very least they assist in the imaginative reconstruction of policy-makers' values, intentions and goals.

The most ambitious attempt to explain the transformation of welfare in ideological terms remains A.V. Dicey's famous analysis of the supposed transition from individualism to collectivism in British public opinion, which Dicey detected in the period after 1870.[3] Yet historians have almost unanimously concurred in finding Dicey's model misleading and unsatisfactory. At a theoretical level it polarises and caricatures overlapping and related schools of thought; and at an empirical level it grossly underestimates both the collectivising strain in *early* Victorian welfare provision, and the vigorous survival of various types of individualism into the twentieth century. More recent historians have concentrated much more closely than Dicey upon the detailed exegesis of ideas about social welfare, and upon situating both theory and policy within a precise historical context. Over the past 40 years a very fertile literature has explored the relationship between changing social policies and such theoretical stances as Utilitarianism, Idealism, Marginalism, Progressivism, Social Darwinism, Marxism, Keynesianism and theories of business management. Many illuminating and often unexpected perspectives have emerged from these studies, reshaping conventional wisdom. Benthamism, for instance, characterised by Dicey as a predominantly individualist philosophy, has been revealed as the seed-bed of the Victorian 'welfare state'.[4] Mid-Victorian social scientists, functioning in the supposed heyday of administrative laissez-faire, have emerged as overwhelmingly in favour of certain kinds of ameliorative state intervention (albeit on somewhat limited and class-specific terms).[5] Eugenics theory, once viewed as the characteristic stronghold of the hard-line radical right, has been convincingly reinterpreted as a much more widely pervasive philosophy shared with socialism and progressive liberalism.[6] The 1909 Poor Law Commission, classically portrayed by Beatrice Webb as a battleground between socialist and individualist ideals, has been recast as a conflict of a very different kind: a conflict in which the rationalising, modernising and professionalising instincts of the Webbs appear to have differed very little from those of their arch-enemies, the adherents of 'voluntarism' and 'family casework' in the Charity Organisation Society.[7] At the same time, the statistical and social-scientific bases of social policy have been systematically scrutinized and shown in many cases to have been underpinned by hidden purposes and ideological preconceptions.[8] Increasingly the very subject-matter of social welfare policy has been redefined as theoretically problematic and contentious. 'Health', 'unemployment', 'poverty' and so on appear no longer as fixed, objective and self-explanatory social phenomena, but as relativistic and socially constructed concepts within the shifting boundaries of the history of ideas.[9]

Such studies have made historians aware that ideas about 'social welfare' can migrate unexpectedly across the political spectrum, and that preconceived assumptions about the left/right implications of particular policies are often false. Precise scholarship can preclude wider perspectives, however, and no recent historian has yet succeeded in substituting a general, empirically based, long-term interpretation of trends in social welfare comparable with that of Dicey. Moreover large areas in the history of ideas about social policy remain almost wholly uncharted. In this article I shall attempt to fill in one of these gaps by surveying some of the professional and semi-professional literature that appeared in Britain on problems of social policy between the 1890s and 1940s—focusing particularly on the theme of changing perceptions of public-private relationships. This survey can make no pretence of comprehensiveness, and will deal primarily with the views of members of the academic, professional and administrative middle classes. I hope, however, to throw light upon changing attitudes to the state, and to draw out certain major themes that have been largely neglected or misinterpreted in the history of twentieth-century social reform.

Social Science and Social Reform

Mid-Victorian Britain had a widely flourishing culture of popular 'social science', operating through the medium of national and local sociological and statistical associations, which carried out extensive inquiries into such questions as health, housing, crime, prostitution and the condition of the poor. The intellectual and political milieux of these societies have been the subject of detailed historical research, and it is well known that their approach to social analysis was highly positivist in methodology and meliorist in its goal.[10] Though going far beyond the poor law in their social interests, they nevertheless largely accepted the framework of atomistic sociology and hedonistic psychology that formed the bases of the principles of 1834. Their social vision was dominated by the belief that middle-class progress could be universalised; and they were an important expression of the booming liberal culture of the mid-Victorian years. Their rationale and organisational cohesion, however, appeared to collapse during the 1880s in the face of economic recession, the growing radical and socialist critique of orthodox liberalism, and widening divisions of social class. Thereafter it is often assumed that their critical role in British society was taken over by political, administrative and 'expert' bodies,[11] and by the growing professionalisation of social-research techniques. This assumption is at least partly incorrect. It is true that social policy became much more formally institutionalised in government departments, that social science began to be studied in universities, and that skills such as statistics, casework, psychology and public-health administration became increasingly defined and organised by professional groups. But this change did not occur overnight. On the contrary, it began almost imperceptibly, and worked itself out very gradually over the next half-century. It was accompanied not by the disappearance, but by the re-emergence and reformulation of a popular and voluntaristic social-scientific culture that in both personnel and social purpose was strikingly similar to that of the mid-Victorian years.

This new movement found expression through a variety of channels: through numerous local Charity Organisation Societies (always research and 'propaganda' bodies as well as promoters of practical casework); through socialist organisations such as the Fabian Society and the Independent Labour Party; through the London and provincial ethical societies; through the university extension and settlement movements; and through the emergence in the 1900s of a range of new civic associations devoted to the advancement of social research and the 'modernisation' of social policy. Prominent among these new bodies were the British Institute of Social Service, the Personal Service Association, the Guild of Help movement, and the numerous civic trusts, councils of social welfare and Elberfeld societies that were set up during the Edwardian period in many British cities and towns.[12] For many people membership of religious social welfare organisations, Protestant, Catholic and Jewish, offered a similar medium of civic concern; and it is worth noting that—far from being sealed off from one another—the membership of socialist, philanthropic, denominational and civic-reform associations in the Edwardian period and later often overlapped.[13] Such organisations were given an immense impetus by the great national debate on the Royal Commission on the Poor Laws after 1909. The national conferences on the prevention of destitution which followed the Commission clearly mobilized and brought into public dialogue a very wide cross-section of informed opinion on questions of social welfare—an opinion that to a large extent transcended the divisions expressed in the Minority and Majority Reports of the Commission.[14] This activity cannot be seen as a mere amateur residue of an earlier interest in scientific social reform that had now largely migrated to a separate public and professional sphere. On the contrary, professional administrators and social scientists were widely active in the new social reform organisations; and, far from being estranged from the new 'academic' culture of the social sciences, civic social reform organisations were often the roots from which sprang the endowment of chairs and departments of social science in London, Scotland and the provincial universities.[15] Moreover this was as true in the field of theoretical and speculative sociology as in the more practical and mundane spheres of social administration and casework. Many of the activists in the new social service and civic reform associations were the very same people who attended the meetings and conferences of the Sociological Society, founded by Victor Branford and Professor Patrick Geddes in 1904 (indeed to many people Geddes was the hero and unofficial high priest of the civic-reform movement).[16] As will be shown in more detail below, one of the most striking features of 'social reform' literature over the next 30 years was to be the continuing interaction between sociological theory, social philosophy, empirical investigation, casework and the analysis of practical social policy. Relations between reformers and investigators and between 'philosophers' and 'scientists' were often stormy; but, in marked contrast to developments in the social sciences after 1945, much of the study of British society in the early decades of the twentieth century continued to form, no less than in the high Victorian period, an interlocking seamless web.[17]

The Triumph of Idealism

The history of these Edwardian social-scientific and social reform organisations, and of their role in both civic culture and the making of social policy, deserves more attention than I have space for here.[18] The same is true of the founding of 'social science' departments in British universities (no less than ten such departments were set up between 1904 and 1919).[19] For the rest of this article I shall largely confine myself to an analysis of their published literature, and to what it tells us about the framework of social and political thought within which developments in social policy took place during the early decades of the twentieth century. How far was there a coherent body of informed opinion about issues of social welfare, as arguably there had been in the mid-Victorian period? And what does the analysis of such opinion reveal about the underlying philosophy of social reform—about approaches to the methodology of the social sciences, the reception of new forms of knowledge, the definition of 'social justice' and the relationship between the individual, society and the state?

The first thing that strikes the reader of this new wave of social reform literature is that, in marked contrast to comparable writing in the mid-Victorian period, much early twentieth-century social science was predominantly 'idealist' in character; idealist, not necessarily in a formal philosophical or methodological sense, but in more general inspiration and tone.[20] The permeation of Edwardian public administration by the political thought of T.H. Green is of course a familiar theme in the history of social policy; but the Idealist infiltration of the governing élite was merely the tip of a much larger iceberg than has usually been acknowledged. Moreover the Idealist frame of reference became even more powerful and all-encompassing in the period *after* the First World War, when for a time at least the earlier traditions of Positivism and Empiricism virtually faded out of large areas of the vocabulary of social science. The cultural hegemony of Idealism was established at many different levels. It was apparent in popular as well as in academic studies, and it was found not merely in abstract treatises on political thought, but in statistical and descriptive studies of concrete social problems, whose subject-matter and methodology appeared on their face to be quite the reverse of Idealist.[21] Its influence was apparent also among evolutionary and functionalist sociologists, who are often portrayed as resistant to the Idealist embrace.[22] This is not, of course, to suggest that, unlike their Victorian predecessors, Edwardian and post-Edwardian social scientists turned their backs on biological and natural-scientific models; but they were increasingly aware of the traps and limitations of those models —and increasingly inclined to view society neither as a machine nor as a physical organism, but as a 'spiritual personality' with a 'moral will'. Evolution, both natural and social, was widely viewed not as a merely material process, but as a dialectical progression towards a moral and spiritual ideal; an ideal, moreover, whose identity was moving ever onward and upward as society advanced.

The sources of this change in the fundamental categories of social thought are not fully apparent, but it was influenced by revolt against the mechanistic theories of the poor-law era, by the absorption of certain aspects of continental Idealism, and by the search for a 'modernist' reformulation of (or an ethical substitute for) traditional Christianity. Moreover the shift towards Idealism from more positivistic modes of thought was often complex and untidy. Numerous Edwardian social theorists such as the Webbs, J.A. Hobson, L.T. Hobhouse and many members of the Sociological Society found themselves painfully caught between two schools—attracted by the altruism, organicism and ethical rationality of Idealism, but confused and sceptical about Idealist methodology and about its emphasis upon the real corporate identity of society and the state. The Idealist school was strongly entrenched, however, among Edwardian academics and professional philosophers; and Idealist professors of philosophy such as Bernard Bosanquet, Edward Urwick, J.H. Muirhead, Henry Jones and James Seth were key figures in the setting up of new university departments of social science. It was they who designed the curricula, wrote the text books and gave the lectures by which the first generation of academically trained social workers and social scientists were taught. Urwick, in particular, as first head of the department of social science and administration at the London School of Economics, was of crucial importance in determining that the core discipline of that department should be not 'social science', not 'sociology', but 'social philosophy'—by which he meant the evaluation of social institutions in the light of a 'pattern' of immutable ethical truths.[23] Urwick's example was subsequently emulated by many other departments of social science in Britain and throughout the British Empire.[24] It was also powerfully mediated by academic social theorists to the civic social reform movement. As one of

Urwick's successors at the London School of Economics, J. St. John Heath, wrote in the house journal of the British Institute of Social Service:

> the real aim of all social reform is so to alter the material conditions of life that man's spiritual faculties may have room for full play, and if this be so the first and foremost object of study must be that of the relation of man's spiritual nature to his material environment.[25]

As I have shown elsewhere, this approach was far more influential in the early days of the development of social science at the LSE than the more mundane descriptive Positivism often associated with the Webbs.[26]

What were the consequences of the popular triumph of Idealism for the intellectual context of British social policy? One point that should be made clear is that, although Idealism has often been equated with reaction and conservatism, it did not create a single political orthodoxy within either the academic departments of social science or the social reform associations. Idealists, both academic and lay, included members of the Liberal, Labour and Conservative parties, supporters and opponents of the Minority Report on the poor laws, enthusiasts for and stern critics of the fashionable science of eugenics.[27] In spite of its emphasis on speculative theory, systematic Idealism did not discourage empirical social research, but claimed that facts were meaningless without an explanatory framework derived from subjective experience and *a priori* reasoning.[28] What it did do, however, was to subordinate the analysis of specific social problems to a vision of reconstructing the whole of British society, together with reform of the rational understanding and moral character of individual British citizens. Social policy was not viewed as an end in itself, nor were the recipients of welfare ends in themselves; on the contrary, both policies and people were means to the end of attaining perfect justice and creating the ideal state. Such a goal may appear to many late twentieth-century eyes as at best vacuous and at worst dangerously authoritarian; but this latter inference sits uneasily with the fact that the vast majority of British Idealists were unremitting enthusiasts for 'active citizenship' and popular democracy. In order to understand more clearly what was meant by the 'ideal state', we need to look more closely at the specific context and content of sociological Idealism and its aspirations and goals.

The Influence of Plato

The Idealist movement is often equated with the influence of Hegel, and certainly many British philosophers and social scientists at the end of the nineteenth century were familiar with, and attracted by, Hegelian ideas, even if only superficially.[29] The literature under review suggests, however, that at least in the context of social science and social policy Hegel was rarely more than a transient and marginal point of reference.[30]Among 'modern' influences he was vastly outweighed by Rousseau (deplored by the Victorians as a subversive lunatic, but rehabilitated by the Edwardians into the moral godfather of the democratic state).[31] And far more potent than any modern theorist as a source of Idealist social thought was classical Greek philosophy, above all the philosophy of Plato. This fact is perhaps unsurprising, given the continued entrenchment of classical studies in British universities and public and secondary schools, and the tremendous revival of academic interest that had been taking place since the 1870s in the translation and scholarly exegesis of Plato's works.[32] But what is more surprising is the extent to which early twentieth-century social scientists found in Plato not simply a system of logic and epistemology, but a series of clues, principles and practical nostrums with which to approach the problems of mass, urban, class-based, industrial and imperial civilisation.[33] Later critics of Idealism such as R.H. Crossman and Karl Popper pointed to the powerful strains of élitist, racialist and eugenic thought in many of Plato's works, and concluded that the revival of Platonism had been a powerful incubator of twentieth-century authoritarianism.[34] But although British Platonists undeniably included a handful of authoritarian theorists (such as the social psychologist, William McDougall),[35] the vast majority of them were reformers, democrats and egalitarians, largely oblivious of Plato's apparent endorsement of absolute political obedience, a functional caste system, and the selective breeding of a governing race. Where such features of Plato's thought *were* noted, they were often glossed over as symbolic, mythical or historically specific to Plato's own time. Bosanquet's *A Companion to Plato's Republic*, for example, ascribed Plato's proposals for the abolition of the family—an institution much extolled by most Edwardian Idealists—to the corrupt condition of family life in fifth-century Sparta:

It is not altogether surprising that Plato, not seeing his way to the combined freedom and dutifulness of the modern family at its best, which is still very far from general realisation, should have suggested putting an end to the system.[36]

What then were the aspects of Plato's thought that made him possibly the most influential, and certainly the most frequently cited, social and political thinker in the sociological and reformist writings of the early twentieth century? A major attraction was Plato's emphasis on society as an organic spiritual community, a conception that happily chimed both with much traditional conservative thought and with new liberal and progressive notions of society as a manifestation of 'mind in evolution'. A second factor was Plato's vision of the ethical nature of citizenship; a vision in which individual citizens found happiness and fulfilment not in transient sensory satisfactions, but in the development of 'mind' and 'character' and in service to a larger whole. A third aspect, particularly attractive to radical liberals and ethical socialists, was Plato's focus on justice rather than force as the basis of the state. And a fourth attraction to some (though not all) British Idealists was Plato's mysticism and anti-materialism—his belief that the totality of truth was supra-social and transcendent, and that life in any given society was merely a transient and largely illusory phase in the 'thousand-year journey of the soul'.[37]

Such perceptions may seem remote from the mundane and material issues of social administration. Yet they crop up with startling regularity in the practical and theoretical literature of early twentieth-century social reform. Bosanquet's lectures specifically grounded the role of the modern social worker in Plato's conception of the statesman. Both relied on 'vision' rather than technical skill, and both were charged with 'bringing the social mind into order, into harmony with itself'.[38] Urwick made Plato the lynchpin of his lectures to students at the Charity Organisation Society's School of Sociology and later at the London School of Economics; and his studies of social philosophy commended Plato's *Republic* as an ethical and visionary guide to government and social policy for the twentieth century.[39] Tom Jones, lecturer in economics at Aberystwyth, and assistant commissioner to the Royal Commission on the Poor Laws, urged acceptance of the Commission's Minority Report on the ground that it embodied 'the Platonic conception of the state as an educational establishment'.[40] The pages of *Progress*, the house journal of the Institute of Social Service, resounded with Idealist, organicist and Platonic themes, such as 'corporate life' as the basis of 'social virtue', social work as a form of 'statesmanship', and promotion of 'social conditions favourable to good citizenship in future generations—a true aristocracy, the Rule of the Best'. The journal's editor was Percy Alden, a progressive liberal, pacifist and Congregationalist minister, who by no stretch of the imagination could be seen as the protagonist of a holistic authoritarian state.[41]

The same frame of reference, often amplified by citation of Aristotle, Herodotus and other Hellenic writers, recurred in many other social-scientific and philosophical journals of the period. Contributors to the *International Journal of Ethics*, for many years a leading organ of the Anglo-American reformist intelligentsia, claimed that 'even those who have not even heard the names of Plato and Aristotle, are, nevertheless, under the spell of their authority'.[42] The *Sociological Review*, strongly committed to the 'modernist' metaphysic of Geddes, nevertheless frequently invoked Hellenic ideals and theories—and, indeed, saw them as perfectly compatible with Geddes' vision of a rational, organic 'Eutopia'. Articles in the review, for long the major journal of British academic sociology, urged writers on 'civics' and political thought 'to present the figures of Pericles or Edwin Chadwick as models for modern youth'.[43] The collapse of fourth-century Hellenic culture was held out as a guide and object-lesson to modern social reformers. The fate of Athens demonstrated:

> the fading of the vivid and highly differentiated life of the city-state into a formless, cosmopolitan society, with no roots in the past and no contact with a particular region.[44]

The *Social Service Review*, founded in 1919 by the National Council for Social Service, portrayed voluntary social work as:

> a means of governing in the Platonic sense ... which will enable the state to become an aggregate of self-conscious, self-balanced and self-preserving units as it ought to be.[45]

Even the social-survey movement, apparently the antithesis of all that Idealism stood for, was pressed into the service of the Platonic state. Involvement in social surveys, particularly on the large anonymous new housing estates of the post-1918 era, was urged as a means of helping citizens:

to enter into community life and to catch some of the gleam which must have inspired Thucidydes when he put the Funeral Oration into the mouth of his Prince ... Maybe we shall in this way help to make democracy in our time the living thing it was for a little while in Athens, 2,500 years ago; enlightened self-rule by ordinary folk.[46]

Similar arguments were used by protagonists of social 'planning', such as Basil Blackett. The tension in planning between freedom and state direction would be resolved, not by the abandonment of democracy, but by Plato's vision of a 'higher type of democracy', based on a corporate moral life.[47] The symbolic climax of the classical model came perhaps in 1931, with an edition of the *Sociological Review* that was largely devoted to multiple obituaries of Victor Branford, the businessman and philanthropist who had founded the Sociological Society a quarter of a century before. Branford was celebrated in verse and prose as a 'wistful brother to luminous Plato', whose own sociological writings and patronage of the social sciences had sought to transform British society in the early twentieth century into the 'pure Heavenly Pattern' of the 'Dear City of God'.[48]

Idealism and the Boundaries of State Action

How did the establishment of a predominantly Idealist framework of social thought affect perceptions of the state, society and the private individual in the sphere of practical social policy? Because several prominent Idealists belonged to the Charity Organisation Society, and because the Charity Organisation Society opposed the Webbs' proposals in the Minority Report of the Poor Law Commission, it is often supposed that the philanthropic strain in British Idealism was a stronghold of old-fashioned laissez-faire individualism. There are, however, several fallacies in this line of argument. Although the COS harboured within its ranks a number of orthodox political economists and 'strict' poor-law theorists, its social philosophy had never been purely 'individualist' in the atomistic sense of that term.[49] On the contrary, its leading members had a strong conception of the corporate nature of society and of the organic interdependence of its members, and many of them favoured what Helen Bosanquet called 'social collectivism'—by which she meant 'the companionship and assistance' of friendly societies, co-operatives and trade unions rather than 'barren intercourse with poor law officials'.[50]

Moreover Bernard Bosanquet's writings on political philosophy indicated that, far from diminishing or marginalising the role of the state, he viewed the state in a very ambitious and transcendent light, not just as the guarantor of property and order, but as the overlord and final arbiter of culture, education, economics, religion and morals. In Bernard Bosanquet's view it was not the COS but his Fabian opponents who were guilty of 'obsolete individualism', because they 'had no conception of the citizen mind'.[51] How can this grandiose vision of comprehensive state power be reconciled with Bosanquet's opposition to such apparently modest forms of public welfare provision as free school dinners and state old-age pensions? Very simply, Bosanquet's state was not the ramshackle, anomic, utilitarian, paternalist oligarchy of King Edward VII's Britain; it was a republic of free, equal, independent, ethically mature and public-spirited citizens of the kind that had haunted European consciousness ever since it was first mooted in the minds of the sages of fifth-century Athens. This perception is vital to the understanding both of Bernard Bosanquet's political thought and of his and Helen Bosanquet's approach to social policy. It explains why Bosanquet so firmly declared himself a democrat, an egalitarian and a lover of liberty, even though to many hostile critics he appeared the exact opposite. And it explains also the Bosanquets' vision of social welfare not as an end in itself, but as a means to an end—the end of fostering and enhancing the ethical rationality which alone could qualify individuals for a passport to citizenship of the virtuous republic. Thus it was not the material fact of a social welfare benefit that was important, but its inner meaning and context. A benefit was allowable (even a state benefit) if it took place within an ethical context (that is, a reciprocal personal relationship between the giver and receiver) and if its end was rational (that is, the promotion of independent citizenship in the recipient). But it was not allowable, either from the state or from private charity, if it involved a mere mechanical and anonymous transfer of resources from one individual to another, with no element of moral purpose or ethical exchange.[52]

Such an interpretation fits the writings of both Bernard and Helen Bosanquet far more closely than accounts which view them simply as defenders either of pre-industrial paternalism or economic laissez faire. Their aim as social reformers was not to keep the poor in their place, but to force the poor into active and prudent participatory citizenship (there is an obvious echo here of the political thought of Rousseau). This theme of inculcating citizenship as the ultimate goal of social welfare was omnipresent in the departments of social science and social-scientific associations and journals discussed earlier in this article; but many social Idealists, and others who were influenced by Idealist modes of thought, dissented radically from the Bosanquets in their assessment of the desirable practical relationship between the citizen and the state. The Webbs, for example, wholly shared the Bosanquets' belief that private and public virtue were interdependent, that 'state-conscious idealism' was the goal of citizenship, and that social welfare policies should be ethically as well as materially constructive: indeed Sidney once described himself as aiming to do in the social sphere what Rousseau had done in the political.[53] But they claimed that the deviant or needy individual could far more easily be provoked into self-improvement from within the context of state social services than if left to his own unaided efforts. James Seth, Idealist moral philosopher and founder of the department of social science at the University of Edinburgh, went so far as to suggest that state services should be made not only freely available, but compulsory: 'we [should] not only encourage, instead of discouraging, application, but force this treatment even upon the most unwilling'.[54] And, as the post-1909 debates on the prevention of destitution made clear, there were many social Idealists who approached the whole issue of poverty from yet another perspective; who held that state removal of the *causes* of ill-health, low wages, malnutrition and unemployment, would in itself sweep away the material and psychological barriers to ethical self-fulfilment and participation in public life.[55] Many members of the infant Labour Party—James Ramsay Macdonald, R.H. Tawney, Clement Attlee, Arthur Greenwood, even the practical and pragmatic Arthur Henderson—were influenced by, and prominent exponents of, this point of view.[56]

This debate continued unabated into the period after the First World War. Social policy makers and social scientists continued to disagree widely about the precise boundaries of state action, and about the best means of 'stimulating the forces of civic shame and civic pride'.[57] Within the National Council of Social Service there was much unease during the 1920s about the piecemeal expansion of unemployment relief—not on grounds of dogmatic hostility to state intervention, but because relief was being given in a 'mechanical' way without a personalised 'ethical' component.[58] There was undisguised glee in some social work circles about the curtailment of uncovenanted benefit, the extension of means tests and the expenditure cuts of 1931—all of which were seen as reviving the rationale and central importance of casework and voluntary action.[59] But others responded in a quite different way—seeing voluntary work as a useful 'camouflage' with which to smuggle in a much more public and communitarian conception of the role of social service.[60] What is striking, however, is the fact that virtually no major social theorist or writer on social policy of this period dissented from the view that the ultimate sphere of 'welfare' in its widest sense was, or ought to be, the institutions of the state.[61] The 1920s was a period of great vitality and innovation in the sphere of voluntary service and in co-operation between public and voluntary sectors—much of which was defended, not on pragmatic grounds, but as a means of enhancing wider corporate consciousness ('to elevate, develop and intensify the common life').[62] Even the national insurance system, initially condemned by prominent Idealists for bypassing the individual's ethical will, was reinterpreted as a forum of possible citizen participation in the organs of the state. The nineteenth-century view that private life and much of social life constituted a sphere of natural liberty of which the state should take no cognizance was conspicuous by its absence. Indeed specialists in the new fields of personal casework, social psychology and psychotherapy increasingly gave voice to the opposite point of view. The 'abnormal' were those incapable of seeing themselves 'as part of a social whole, with self-realization only to be gained as a member of the whole', wrote the psychologist Alice Raven in the *Sociological Review* for 1929:

> The 'herd' gives them no stimulus, they are detached from social life ... You may see such persons in the street, walking very fast, looking at no one, often carrying a stick or umbrella.[63]

The Crash of Idealism

In a contribution to a book on *Recent Developments in European Thought*, published in 1919, A.D. Lindsay, the future master of Balliol, and himself a prominent teacher of Idealist political theory, remarked that the Idealist school had now established itself virtually beyond the reach of criticism. The 'powerful and malignant theory' of 'scientific individualism' had been swept away into the dustbin of history.[64] This was a rash judgement even in 1919, for Idealism had already passed its zenith among pure philosophers;[65] but it accurately records the all-encompassing impact of Idealism on both academic and popular social and political thought at this time. A quarter of a century later, in the aftermath of the Second World War, Lindsay recorded with some bewilderment the opposite fact—that Idealism in its turn had been ignominiously deposed by various forms of Positivism. British philosophy had turned its back on the theory and practice of politics. Sociological theory had become almost wholly divorced from the promotion of social welfare. The study of ethics in British universities was now reduced to discussing 'the most jog-trot and insignificant facts of moral conduct, such as the necessity of keeping trivial promises or of saving bits of string'.[66]

Why this change had occurred lies largely beyond the scope of this article; but a creeping disenchantment with Idealist forms of discourse as a theoretical framework for social policy can be detected in many quarters from the early 1930s. After the apotheosis of Victor Branford in 1931, the *Sociological Review* and other social-scientific journals swung rapidly away from Idealist and organic thought, and were increasingly taken over by articles that were descriptive, functionalist, Freudian or quasi-Marxian in methodology and tone.[67] The revolt against Idealism that had been lurking in philosophic circles for the previous 20 years burst into a torrent in the mid-1930s with the onset of linguistic positivism; and the speculative discussion of underlying principles that had been such a marked feature of social policy debate over the previous 40 years vanished virtually overnight from the organs of academic philosophy.

Moreover the crash of Idealism was more than just an episode in academic fashion. It took with it much of the intellectual capital of those who had built up the British social services and were in the process of constructing the British welfare state. This was not, of course, fully evident for many years, and much of the public moral discourse about social welfare in the 1940s and 1950s continued to echo Idealist or quasi-Idealist themes.[68] The social policies advocated by William Beveridge, who in social-scientific methodology was an out-and-out positivist, were nevertheless rooted in a vision of state and society that bore all the hallmarks of the Idealist and Hellenistic tradition.[69] The social philosophy of Richard Titmuss, Urwick's apostolic successor as head of the department of social science at the London School of Economics, was full of muffled resonances of the Idealist discourse of the Edwardian age.[70] But, in marked contrast to the Victorian, Edwardian and inter-war periods, writing about social policy after the Second World War bore almost no trace of any input from professional moral philosophers or from social and political theorists. This negative fact was perhaps of little importance during the period when social welfare rode on the crest of a wave of universal popular enthusiasm. But it was likely to be of much greater significance if and when the welfare state fell into disrepute and had to be defended against systematic and fundamental intellectual challenge.

The Legacy of Idealism

What conclusions can be drawn from this review of the intellectual background of modern social policy? What did Idealism contribute to the structural changes in British political and governmental culture noted at the beginning of this article? As I stated earlier, I have no desire to suggest that Idealism or any other form of theory offers the sole key to the twentieth-century transformation of the British state. But the predominance of Idealism—with its emphasis on corporate identity, individual altruism, ethical imperatives and active citizen-participation—meshed and interacted with the mundane working of social policy in Britain during the first half of the twentieth century at many different levels. Idealism permeated the education system at every tier, from the public schools to the state elementary schools, and was at least partly responsible for the powerful anti-vocational bias that characterised British educational institutions for much of the twentieth century. The aim of state schools was 'stimulating fine thought in children and ... making them aspire to what is best and highest in life', declared Professor R.A. Gregory to the education section of the National Conference on the Prevention of Destitution; 'if a Curriculum is desired which will make men and women content with a wretched existence, the Elementary Schools do not provide it and we hope they never will'.[71] The influence of Idealist philosophy was largely responsible for the fact that, by contrast with much of Europe and North America, the academic study of social work and 'social science' developed as humane disciplines within university departments rather than as technical disciplines in independent professional schools. In British training for social work, 'emphasis has always been placed on the right attitude of mind towards Society and its progress rather than methods and operations', wrote a member of the Joint Universities Council for Social Work Training in 1925.[72] As I hope I have shown, however, social Idealism was by no means a closet ideology, confined to a small handful of academics and teachers and intellectuals. It was for a time as popular and pervasive among the socially active middle classes as evangelicalism or utilitarianism had been in the nineteenth century. Those consciously committed to Idealism as an intellectual system were always a small minority; but, as with evangelicalism, they were a potent and articulate minority, whose influence extended far beyond the boundaries of professional social administration and organised social science. Moreover Idealism united people who differed widely on political tactics; it generated a vocabulary of social reform that transcended political parties; and it helps to explain the enthusiasm for, or at least tolerance of, the growth of centralised social services within a political culture that had traditionally been hostile to any accretion of state power. Indeed its influence is particularly striking among the kind of provincial Nonconformist intellectuals who had always been a stronghold of English libertarian individualism. As a Methodist local government official attached to the Manchester Education Committee put it in 1934:

the State has evolved from being the embodiment of force and developed gradually until in modern days it emerges as guide, philosopher and friend.[73]

It is hard to imagine similar sentiments being expressed at that time by his opposite numbers in much of western Europe.

The substantive content of Idealist thought presents difficulties for late twentieth-century historians, hemmed about as we are by a very different cultural and linguistic frame of reference. Much Idealist writing may seem to us either wilfully difficult and obscure or weakly sentimental and self-evident. But any popular political philosophy is liable to lapse into bathos, without thereby impairing its historical significance. My purpose in this article has not been to rehabilitate Idealism, but to uncover its role in providing a popular idiom and legitimizing framework for modern social policy and the growth of the welfare state. Other political theories, such as new liberalism, ethical socialism, 'national efficiency' and the 'national minimum', contribute to this legitimating process; but they were often not so much rivals of Idealist thought as offshoots or partners of it. Even utilitarianism became for a time partly subsumed under the Idealist umbrella, partly through the works of the Fabian Idealist D.G. Ritchie and, less explicitly and more eclectically, in many of the writings of the Webbs.[74]

Quite why Idealism was so successful, albeit for a limited period, in providing a popular vocabulary for social reform must be a matter for speculation. It has been seen by some as a symptom of élitist anti-modernism and retreat into a classical Arcadia, but I do not think that this view can be generally sustained.[75] On the contrary, the concerns of many of its practitioners were strongly 'modernist' and rationalistic; and many of them were firm upholders of the 'contractarian' view of welfare (as opposed to the more archaic belief that rights to welfare were rooted in community and status). Moreover social-scientific Idealism as it had developed by the 1920s was very much the philosophy not of Oxbridge cloisters (where it was by that time distinctly on the wane), but of slum-clearance and new housing estates, town halls and civic universities, the 'England of the arterial roads'. Nor can Idealism simply be dismissed as part of a wider impulse towards state-worship and totalitarian-ism, since—whatever may have been the case in a European context—in Britain most Idealists were strongly committed to activating popular democracy and deeply hostile to the mere mechanical growth of bureaucratic power.

The appeal of Idealism must therefore be sought elsewhere. It must be remembered that British Idealism was addressing itself to what was perhaps the most urbanised, industrialised, and class-stratified society in the world at the time. It was a society, moreover, that was only just in the process of opening itself up to popular democracy, and where the structure of the constitu-tion appeared to indicate that popular control of the franchise would lead inevitably to some degree of popular control of the state. Idealism was a philosophy that attempted to grapple with this transition, by inseminating into what Graham Wallas and others called 'the Great Society' the moral and civic purposes of the Greek city state.[76] It was as much part of what Rodney Lowe has termed 'adjustment to democracy' as the more tangible and pragmatic processes of day-to-day public administration. The invocation of Hellensim, and particularly of Plato, was more than just decorative rhetoric. It was designed to provide a model that would help to re-integrate the fragmented consciousness of modern man into cohesive corporate communities.[77] And it was meant to assist in addressing an age-old, but newly relevant question: how can men live in large groups and yet remain free? Social policy and the provision of social services were, according to Idealist social philosophers, inextricably bound up in the answer to this question; hence the emphases on 'citizenship' and 'social service', not just as modes of distributing and rationing material resources, but as part of the higher moral life of the state. Hence also the emphasis on 'character', which (however grotesquely misapplied at times in day-to-day social-work practice) was meant to act not as a moral means test, but as a stimulus to independence and political emancipation.

The vulnerable points of such a theory are in retrospect overwhelmingly obvious, as they were to many critical contemporaries—the glossing-over of structural inequalities, the lack of adequate reference to a framework of class, the optimistic assumptions about corporate national identity, the neglect of the intransigent facts of human diversity and conflict. A fundamental weakness was the divorce of Idealism from British economic thought, which throughout the period covered by this paper was for the most part moving in a strongly positivistic direction. Attempts by A.C. Pigou and others to smuggle certain Idealist preconceptions into neo-classical political economy through the medium of 'welfare economics' remained largely extraneous both to the mainstream of economic thought and to practical thinking about social policy.[78] But these objections do not alter the fact that Idealism was the overarching philosophy of the early days of the welfare state; nor the fact that subsequent theorists of welfare have been conspicuously unsuccessful in constructing any more coherent, plausible and morally compelling alternative.

The Poor Law Reports of 1909 and the Social Theory of the Charity Organisation Society

A.W. Vincent

Majority and Minority Reports

IT is a characteristic feature of writing about the Royal Commission on the Poor Laws, which sat between 1905 and 1909, to establish a firm distinction between the Minority and Majority Reports, to maintain that the Minority Report was the forward looking and prophetic document, and to dismiss the main ideas of the Majority as a hangover from nineteenth century ideology. Whereas the political campaigning of the National Committee for the Break-up of the Poor Law ensured the reputation of the Minority Report, the Majority Report, as Michael Rose has remarked, 'was pushed into obscurity'.[1] The Majority 'came to be seen increasingly as a mere reactionary defender of the status quo'.[2] Many still concur with the view that 'the Majority Report of the Royal Commission on the Poor Laws ... still smacked of individualism'.[3] One of the key reasons for this judgement is that the Majority Report on the Poor Law has very strong associations with the Charity Organisation Society, which is seen as the archetypal expression of nineteenth-century individualism.

Opinions have differed on the role and influence of the Charity Organisation Society; there are four basic views which can be clearly delineated. The strongest and most traditional interpretation has been to see the Charity Organisation Society (hereafter referred to as the COS) as a purely reactionary individualist organisation, little different from groups like the Liberty and Property Defense League. Seebohm Rowntree took this line in

---

This chapter first appeared as an article in *Victorian Studies*, Vol. 27, No. 3, Spring 1984, pp. 343-63 and is reproduced here by permission.

1901 in response to COS criticism of his work on poverty. Beatrice Webb also accused the COS of consisting of laissez-faire individualists, critical of all governmental extension.[4] Asa Briggs echoed this position in his study of Rowntree in 1961.[5] He commented that the COS 'were strong individualists, critical of "the foolish charity of the public" and shocked by what they regarded as the "horrible cruelty of the sentimental interference with the lives of the poor"'.[6] The resistance to government action on poverty, the espousal of free market economics, the distinction between the deserving and undeserving poor, and the opposition to social legislation are seen as the characteristic features of COS individualism.

A second line of interpretation, however, has been adopted from the 1940s on. This interpretation is premised on a clear distinction between the ideology of individualism and the actual social work practice. Whereas the ideology is dismissed as anachronistic, the social work practice is seen as looking toward developments in the twentieth century. This position has been taken by William H. Beveridge, Maurice Bruce, T.H. Marshall, David Owen, Michael Rose, Robert Pinker, and Derek Fraser, amongst others.[7] Marshall and Owen acknowledge their difficulty in dealing seriously with so repugnant an ideology.[8] Rose sums up this position in his comment:

> With its stern insistence on individualism and self-help, its rejection of state aid except in a minor role and its distinction between the deserving and the undeserving poor, it might seem to epitomise all that was worst in the Victorian attitude to the poor ... Yet despite these attitudes, most historians of social policy agree that the COS had a valuable contribution to make.[9]

The valuable contribution of the COS for all these historians lay primarily in the field of casework, specifically family casework, and less significantly in the training of social workers.

This interpretation has been criticised by Gareth Stedman Jones, who argues that the individualist ideology is not distinct from the social casework.[10] Theory and practice were united; they stood or fell together. For Stedman Jones, to understand the COS we need to refer to their social class background and ambitions. They institutionalised the fears of a professional, wealthy middle class who were attempting to 'reintroduce the element of obligation into the gift'.[11] The COS consisted also of an aspiring urban gentry who wanted a hierarchical and deferential society.

The emphasis placed on thorough casework and social work training was part and parcel of their professional self-image, situating the casework perspective within the ideological framework.

Character and Poverty

The argument of this paper follows Stedman Jones' insight that the social casework activities of the COS cannot be separated from its individualistic social theory. Along with many other earlier historians, however, Stedman Jones has fundamentally misunderstood the nature of this social theory, specifically the idea of its individualism. Many COS ideas were fluid enough to allow a subtle transformation of COS policies towards a greater acceptance of state activity. This point can be observed by examining the various arguments surrounding the 1909 Poor Law Reports. The Minority Report, which was essentially a Fabian document constructed by Beatrice Webb, is often seen as the forerunner of more modern attitudes to poverty. This paper aims to show first that the Majority Report was not a manifestation of individualism *simpliciter*, and second, that the Majority Report encapsulated a more complex social theory than is often realised. Despite being more questionable on theoretical grounds, the Majority Report was a more honest document, reflecting the intrinsic tensions underlying discussions of poverty. It would also be an extreme simplification to say that the Minority Report was a forward-looking document. It too reflected many themes from the previous century. I admit that the COS treatment of the poor was at times harsh and uncompromising and that some of their workers had rather crude notions of self-help and character deficiency. To stress these negative features of the COS, however, can easily lead to caricature; a different picture emerges by giving equal stress to those COS figures who presented a coherent, thoroughly articulated social vision and tried to put it into practice.

Beatrice Webb wrote in her second autobiographical account, *Our Partnership*, that the contending sides of the poor law dispute were those who supported the Minority Report, including the Liberal press, organised labour, officials of the preventive services, and a section of the public, and those who rejected it, including the medical profession, the 'relief of distress' philanthropists and their voluntary aid committees, and the Hegelians, led by Bernard Bosanquet.[12] As the Minority Report encapsulated the social theories of the Webbs, so likewise did the Majority Report embody the views of the COS. Bernard Bosanquet had claimed in 1910 that the Majority Report represented part of the COS 'social vision'.[13] Charles Loch Mowat, the historian of the society, agreed, stating that the Majority Report 'represented substantially the Charity Organisation Society point of view': the 'Majority Report remains of interest as the ultimate embodiment of the idea of charity organisation as preached and practised by the Charity Organisation Society'.[14] The Webbs had also expressed some of their central theories in the Minority Report, which Beatrice Webb claimed had 'a philosophic basis in the whole theory of the enforced minimum'.[15] The reports in principle can be said to represent two contrasting philosophical approaches to the problem of poverty.

Most of the prominent signatories to the Majority Report were COS members; I will assume that the key spokespersons of the society were two of these signatories, Helen Bosanquet and the COS president C.S. Loch, and also the non-signatory, Bernard Bosanquet. It must be admitted that these particular figures may not represent the COS *in toto*. Bernard Bosanquet and his wife Helen had themselves pointed this out in an article in the *Contemporary Review*.[16] As *The Times* newspaper remarked on Loch's death in 1923, however, C.S. Loch 'made the Charity Organisation Society, he was the Charity Organisation Society'.[17] He was generally regarded by many to be the indisputable head and dominant personality of the society, especially through its polemical years. He was also in basic agreement with the views of his friend Bernard Bosanquet, who was the society's preeminent apologist and theoretician. Loch and Bosanquet had become friends while students of T.H. Green at Balliol College, and Bosanquet dedicated his most famous work, *The Philosophical Theory of the State*, to Loch.[18] Although these three may not have been representative of the entire spectrum of COS opinion, they were the most theoretically articulate, and can be said to have formulated the most complete picture of the society's purpose. The views which these three represented were based on philosophical Idealism. This is a fact which many historians seem to have missed, and yet it is of considerable importance for judging the COS notion of individualism and the theoretical underpinnings of the Majority Report.

The main proposals of both reports may be briefly summarised in order to put the debate in context. The Majority Report argued for a national system of labour exchanges, a public assistance statutory authority, public assistance committees, and voluntary aid committees. These latter committees were envisaged as working co-operatively. The ideas put forward in the Goschen Minute of 1869, which advised co-operation between guardians and voluntary charitable societies, were to be generalised and enforced. All charities would have to register with the voluntary aid committees, and persons not relieved or helped by these would be automatically referred to a public assistance committee. Apart from the separate treatment of the unemployed, it thus proposed a dualistic arrangement, which many of its critics and supporters understood to mean a reinvigorated poor law and a reinforced COS, with different names. One of the key functions of the COS from the 1870s forward had been to organise, centralise, and systematise charity, and this function was given new emphasis in the Majority Report.

The Minority Report, apart from agreeing with the Majority Report that the 1834 Poor Law should be reformed, argued for the creation of a registrar of public assistance, the total break-up of the 1834 model, and the establishment of a pluralistic range of committees dealing separately with different categories of destitution, for example, children, the sick, the mentally defective, and the aged. The idea of a single category of poverty was to be abandoned. The 'able-bodied' were to be treated by a ministry of labour, again as a separate unit from the bodies responsible for the sick, the old, and the handicapped. Unemployment was often the result of events totally beyond the control of the individual; therefore it should not be treated as merely another aspect of poverty. Both reports agreed on a penal system of work camps for the intractable 'residuum', that is to say those who refused to perform any work. The Webbs conceived of their Minority Report as a total break with the past: it expressed their doctrine of the enforced minimum in society, through which no one would be allowed to fall below a primary poverty line. The pluralistic structure of committees was envisaged as undermining the stigma attached to destitution in general. Welfare was to be put on a scientific, collectivist basis.[19]

The general criticism made by the Majority was that the Minority Report ignored independence of character. No matter how many committees dealt with an individual, the Majority believed, it was quite often a failure of will and character which was at the root of destitution. Independence of character was essential for overcoming poverty. Financial difficulty was not always due to educational deficiency, bad health, or market fluctuations. Some of the poor needed specialised casework from specialised voluntary bodies, presumably like the COS. The number of committees proposed by the Minority was also taken to task as producing a multiplicity of overlapping bodies. The Minority's method of approach, it was claimed, ignored the essential social and restorative role of the family. Further criticism centred upon the suggestions for expansion of free treatment and public expenditure on welfare.

The Minority answered these criticisms by stating that the idea of independence of character, which they called the moral factor of destitution, was only restoring the old idea of deterrence. Under its rather dubious cloak, the sick, the aged, the mentally defective, and children were to be lumped together as paupers. The 'multiplicity of bodies' argument was denied by stating that each officer would know his particular sphere—for example, children or the aged—and that this would diminish the risk of overlapping. The family, the Minority Report argued, was disintegrating because preventive help was not forthcoming. Specialised committees would take seriously the importance of keeping families intact. The public expenditure involved would eventually lessen, since more effective prevention and cure would be achieved. The Minority further criticised the potential over-lapping in the Majority proposals, between, for example, the existing publicly organised hospitals and the projected facilities for health care. The voluntary system of charitable organisation was also attacked as licensing irresponsible amateurs, a point which must have particularly galled the COS.

The intention here is not to enter into a detailed examination of the reports but rather to present a brief overview and then to focus on some of the key arguments. These arguments revolve around the ideas of character, the causes of poverty, and the role of state intervention. The attitudes expressed by the two reports on these ideas embody the central dichotomies between the two social theories. It will therefore be instructive at this point to focus on the explicit defence offered for each of the reports.

Bernard Bosanquet's article 'The Reports of the Poor Law Commission' in the *Sociological Review* was taken by his opponents as summing up the majority's case.[20] Bosanquet regarded

the two reports as having interpreted events differently. Whereas
the Majority regarded the evils of the present system as arising
from the failure of earlier reforms and reformers to adjust to new
demands and conditions, the Minority felt the evils were inherent
in the system itself. The Majority wanted to remove hindrances,
the Minority to break up the system. The aim of the Majority was
to provide help that was preventive, curative, and restorative.
This was to be implemented by the dual organs of the public
assistance and the voluntary aid committees, which corre-
sponded, in Bosanquet's article, to the distinction between the
problem of habitual poverty and the normal provisions for health,
education, and temporary relief. Another way of putting this
distinction was in terms of sheer misfortune and an unwillingness to engage in employment. As Bosanquet commented
elsewhere: 'The Lancashire cotton famine was a great deal easier
to handle than the conditions of chronic semi-employment and
the ins-and-outs'.[21] Helen Bosanquet reformulated this distinction as the difference between the unwilled incapacity and wilful
incapacity for work. As she argued:

> In drawing a distinction between those who are driven to seek public
> assistance by temporary misfortune and those who habitually rely
> upon it, the commission has made a new departure.[22]

New departure or not, the distinction was central and cannot be
dismissed as a verbose way of speaking of the deserving and
undeserving poor. Charity was an essential aspect of what the
Bosanquets called 'civilised group life'. It forged a path between
the caprice of total independence and state organisation. Bernard
Bosanquet argued that charity, conceived of as organised
voluntary action, was a principal social laboratory. Institutions
would grow through this type of creative work. Organised
voluntary charity, by which the COS meant systematic casework
by trained social workers, backed up by centralised funds from
voluntary sources, was essentially for those with an unwilled
incapacity for work. It was to be regarded as an equal partner
with the public assistance committee, which dealt with the willed
incapacity of those who would not help themselves. In reply to
the Minority's criticism that non-elected voluntary bodies were
undemocratic, Bosanquet adopted a characteristic ploy. He
argued that, in effect, traditional elective democracies rely on
crude controls which manifest the 'will of all', an aggregate of
individual interests. Mature democracies, however, rely upon the

'general will' and the moral independence of individuals and groups. Democracies, he argued:

> are beginning to feel the truth of this; that is, to recognise the value of independent and comparatively permanent organs of their will, such as the one great traditional example—the English judiciary.[23]

Bosanquet envisaged the COS and public assistance committees as part of this democratic maturity and general will. He accused the Minority of suffering under the delusions of a defective social theory. Charity as he conceived of it, moreover, was not a gift, but in a sense was the right of the individual citizen. This position divorced it from most of the conceptions of charity discussed in the nineteenth century. It was a right, however, which implied certain responsibilities not only by the community but also by the recipient. The responsibility of the recipient was to submit to the social-scientific casework investigation of voluntary organisations, and by and large to follow their advice. This COS idea was often criticised as legitimating the activity of 'nosey' detectives and 'busy-bodies'.

The principal innovative proposal of the Majority Report, as far as Bernard Bosanquet was concerned, was the role of the voluntary aid committees, which were to employ what Bosanquet called 'social therapeutics'. The principle behind social therapeutics was 'respect for the self-maintaining character'.[24] Failure in social terms, namely poverty, was seen as a failure of self-maintenance in the character of the person. The failure was a moral one since it involved the individual's inability to look to the common social good. Many became destitute due to the instability of trade cycles and changes in techniques of production. These could be fairly simply dealt with, presumably after a screening by a voluntary aid committee. Before the Majority Report, the COS had in fact pioneered the separate treatment of cases not covered by the poor law. They had always treated temporary unemployment differently, and they were also active in the separate treatment of the mentally defective, the blind, and the sick. In the COS estimation, however, some individuals needed more than just temporary help, health care, or the three Rs. There were some who needed detailed casework. Social therapeutics was concerned with the whole person, the individual who needed individualised help from trained social workers. This point became virtually a COS motto—the 'one-by-one' method. This was connected to a broader issue in COS theory. For the

COS there was no general class of the poverty-stricken. Rather each person had to be treated separately as a unique case with an individual range of problems. Bosanquet's social vision, like that of Loch, was one of a scientific charity—a friendly army, as Loch put it, of trained social workers, helping individuals to fulfil their social obligations.[25] The aim of such social work was to enable individuals to realise the common good. Whether all individual cases were curable, however, remained an ambiguous point. The role of the 'residuum' presented a serious problem. This was the group who, in COS terms, remained obdurately or wilfully in poverty, no matter what help they received. Were these to be referred to the public assistance committees? One suspects that this shifting group was to be subject to the penal detention colonies advocated in both reports.

The cure of the whole person remained the central concern of the Majority. As one commentator on the Minority Report put it:

offering the administrators segments of *homo sapiens* rather than entire human beings, made it difficult for them to remember the humanity and dignity of the people they were regulating ... Mrs Webb knew that the study of human relations was necessary for the survival of modern society: but for all her faith in scientific method and in specialists, she was a prisoner of categories and failed to see that casework was a specialism.[26]

In the Majority Report, the COS should be concerned (where poverty arose) with the whole person and not merely with segments of the problem. In fact there is a peculiar fallacy here relating to the idea of overlapping, which was one of the principal criticisms by the Minority of the Majority. The Webbs' method was to relate the problem that any individual might have to specific services, for example those dealing with unemployment, medical care, or lunacy. This was proposed against the older methods of relating all problems to charity and the poor law institutions. With the growth of municipal hospitals and asylums, the Webbs felt that considerable overlap would take place between the municipal and voluntary bodies. But what of the person whose problem was directly related to unemployment, and who consequently was suffering mental distress and illness? Would it be enough to give such a person money? Did the Webbs mean that the specialised bureaucrats they envisaged would not overlap in dealing with unemployment, medical care, and family problems? Was it wise to consider each element of the total problem as isolated? Surely there was a problem of knowing the precise boundaries of each specialism and each particular element? Where would medical, psychological, and financial assistance begin or end? The Majority view was that purely economic help could be adequately provided by the public assistance committees, but that complex social problems ought to be dealt with by voluntary, inventive, yet organised casework, dealing with the whole person and not just elements of the problem. This is the area in which the COS pioneered the idea of family casework, which was their attempt to treat problems in the widest possible context. The whole argument demonstrates that the proposals of the Majority would have entailed far less overlap than the plurality of services suggested by the Minority.

Bernard Bosanquet in other papers saw a specific relationship between Idealist philosophy and COS casework.[27] Both Idealism and the COS version of casework embodied, according to Bosanquet, the vision of reality as a whole. The logic of Idealism and social work was not to be tolerant of one-sided or partial facts, but to investigate the whole problem. As Bosanquet argued:

> Social workers are surely more than anyone familiar with the transfor-
> mation which experience undergoes as more light is thrown upon it
> and fresh points of view emerge... the logic of Idealism—the demand to
> realise unity—is the most disquieting of all ferments.[28]

Social facts, he wrote, 'criticize each other' when compared, because they are all partial aspects of one reality.[29] Casework, like philosophy, must look for some order in the myriad of details. Bosanquet described the process of philosophising as beginning with the appearance of the world and looking through this to the underlying patterns of reality. The same process should take place in casework. Each case should be regarded as unique and in need of thorough investigation. Each individual is a meeting point of a nexus of family, economic, neighbourhood, and general social forces. All of these forces must be taken into account in casework. Such a method Bosanquet would have called, in Hegelian language, utilising the concrete as opposed to relying upon the abstract universal, abstraction being, for an Hegelian, the isolation of components of reality. The concrete is the comprehensive. As Bosanquet commented:

> Our work is nothing but examples of this process, from completing the
> enquiries on a case, to introducing some order into the medical
> charities of London; and to feel and master the way in which imperfect

realities demand to be completed is that very innermost mainspring of life and faith which we call Idealism.[30]

The social worker and the Idealist philosopher are thus spurred by the passion for and logic of reality, which is completeness and wholeness. These ideas lay at the core of the Bosanquets' and Loch's conception of 'thorough charity', involving detailed investigation of case histories, assessing character, social conditions, family, working habits, and so on.[31] This is what Helen Bosanquet and Loch had in mind when they discussed the role of specialised voluntary aid committees.

Bernard Bosanquet, like Loch, argued for an 'army of social healers', trained and united by a common purpose. For the failed will a thorough investigation was needed. The 'revolution' posed by the Majority was built upon the principles of the Poor Law of 1834, which he thought only negatively recognised the virtue of the restored individual. In this sense revolution is probably a misnomer and evolution would be the more appropriate term. The actual treatment of cases, he argued, should have no stigma attached to it. Rather the aim was to restore the capacity for citizenship in all individuals.

The concept of citizenship was a recurring theme in the writings of both Bosanquet and Loch on the COS and Majority Report. As Bosanquet stated in one of his articles, the COS 'start from the ideal of democratic citizenship', which was the core idea behind the COS notion of the individual.[32] Citizenship was also linked to a number of other misunderstood words like character, independence, self-management, and self-maintenance. The notion of individualism in COS writings has been markedly misinterpreted. Beatrice Webb associated the individualism of the COS with laissez-faire economic theories and a consequent dislike of all state intervention,[33] while Robert Pinker associates it with Herbert Spencer: 'Spencer's vigorously individualistic doctrines of self-help found expression in the work of the COS'.[34] But Bosanquet contrasted what he called the ethical individual against the Spencerian atomic individual.[35] The ethical individual was characterised by a development to a high degree of humanity, being self-governing and self-maintaining, and in Hegelian terms was more concrete or comprehensive than atomic. The true ethical individual was also the rational citizen. Self-management and independence implied that the individual was economically self-reliant, but this was the result of a rational disposition rather than a value in itself. Survival in the economic world was ultimately indicative of the survival of the most reasonable; independence was thus revealed with greater clarity at lower wage levels. The hereditary rich managed to obscure their incapacity and lack of independence. As Helen Bosanquet argued, a very high order of intellect was required to be self-supporting on an intermittent income.[36] This independence was also the basis of the COS understanding of character, which implied a positive conception of power in the individual bound up with his or her latent physical and mental capacities. These capacities were seen to be evolving in all individuals, specifically in situations of difficulty and hardship. Character was also seen as a sign of the predominance of rationality. The individual should control and direct his or her own behaviour and inclinations through an awareness of common social purposes embodied in institutions like the family. The individual who determined his or her own actions within social parameters was essentially the rational citizen and was the heart of what Bosanquet called the political maturity of a state, manifesting the general will.

Bosanquet's analysis went deeper than this, however, since the idea of the independent rational citizen implied a theory of mind and will. In another of his defensive articles in 1910, 'Charity Organisation and the Majority Report', Bosanquet defined independence as a 'certain completeness of will and ideas, and outwardly a certain degree of success in the control of circumstances'.[37] Without a certain mental attitude the individual cannot attain outward success. Bosanquet explicitly tied his theory of will and independence to his Idealist philosophy. In one of his philosophical articles, 'The Reality of the General Will', Bosanquet analysed the will as fundamentally the dominant ideas which guide the attention and action of the individual.

For Bosanquet, the individual mind should be 'considered as a machine, of which the parts are ideas or groups of ideas, all tending to pass into action'. The will 'consists of those ideas which are guiding attention and action'.[38] In his definition of the will, Bosanquet directly followed the Idealist tradition. Hegel had defined the will as 'thinking translating itself into existence, thinking is the urge to give itself existence'.[39] He called it, at another point, 'self-determining universality', the will's object being itself.[40] Hegel derived his idea from Immanuel Kant's arguments on the self-legislating will. The moral person is not governed by causal necessity but is conversely autonomous and self-determining. The individual is subject and author of the principles he or she obeys.[41] The Idealist tradition adopted this Kantian theory of the will to show essentially that there is no experience or action apart from that which takes place through the medium of ideas. There could be nothing prior to ideas. As Francis Bradley put it, volition is 'the realization of itself by an idea, an idea ... with which the self here and now is identified, or it is will where an idea with which the self feels itself one, makes its own content to exist'.[42]

For Bosanquet certain ideas had a logical and systematic power to dominate and focus the mind. They enabled the individual to grasp and solve a range of problems. Success in coping with problems reinforced the ideas and the forms of action which flowed from them. Bosanquet thought that such formative ideas reflected the real necessities of human life. He was thinking of notions like social responsibility, caring for one's family and fellow citizens, thrift, foresight, independence of thought, and self-awareness. He maintained that these ideas, which had been reflected on over generations, were derived from the institutions of social life itself. They were 'the inside which reflect the material action and real conditions that form the outside'.[43] Despite the fact that we might now find it odd to think of these ideas as reflecting 'real necessities', Bosanquet considered that they embodied reason. The good will was one in which reason and will were united in certain dominant ideas. They formed the substance to the general will which Bosanquet described as 'the whole working system of dominant ideas which determines the places and functions of its members'.[44] Dominant ideas marshalled the contents of the mind and structured the activity of the agent.

Although Bosanquet was here building up an argument about the general will, it illustrates a central philosophical theme in the COS position. This theme can be understood in terms of the following syllogism. All circumstances and material conditions are created and structured by actions. All actions are structured by the will, which is essentially the dominant ideas of the mind. The corollary of these propositions is that all conditions and circumstances are ultimately the product of and reflect the structure of mind and will, a characteristic Idealist position. One key inference from this conclusion is that in order to change social conditions, it is necessary to change the mind or will. This can be achieved by implanting or substituting new for old dominant ideas, which are marshalling the contents of consciousness; in so doing the will, mind, material circumstances, and ultimately the entire social world can be transformed. Bosanquet's social theories involve a dynamic theory of the will, part of his general Idealist philosophical position. Bosanquet's stress on will gives more substance to remarks like Loch's, in 1910, that charity 'has sought to transform the world by the transformation of will and the inward life of the individual'.[45] The transformation of will was the central function of charity work. No social change could come without such a mental change. Casework charity existed to establish or to help establish the dominant ideas which were the basis of will, and it was the will which structured and was in turn reinforced by social activity. The activity of the individual determined his or her material circumstances and total environment, including work habits, housing, and family life. Charity aimed to establish dominant ideas like thrift, social responsibility, foresight, care of one's family, and independence of mind, which were necessary for the democratic independence of a mature state based on the general will. These ideas were capable of uniting all the disorganised, instinctual faculties of the mind into an organised systematic will. This in turn reinforced the action of the individual, and consequently had a beneficial effect on the material environment. Helen Bosanquet summed up this argument when she stated that 'a man's circumstances depend upon what he himself is; but this does not mean that there is always a conscious choice, that he always knows he is rejecting one circumstance in favour of another. More often he is simply attracted to what interests him, and that depends upon what he already has in his mind. If he has no interests in the higher sense, then his appetites and habits will make his circumstances'. The aim of charity she maintained was to establish new interests 'which will be a clue to guide his life'.[46]

This Idealist theory of will and the ethical individual underpins the Majority Report. As Bosanquet put it:

The Majority proceed upon the principle that where there is a failure of social maintenance ... there is a defect in the citizen-character ... and that therefore every case of this kind raises a problem which is 'moral' in the sense of affecting the whole capacity of self-management, to begin with in the person who has failed, and, secondarily, in the whole community so far as influenced by expectation and example.[47]

There are continual references throughout Bosanquet's and Loch's writings on the COS and Majority to pauperism as a failure in the citizen-mind or character, a failure only thinly disguised in the outwardly wealthy. Throughout its work, and especially in the Majority Report, the COS aimed at strengthening the mind by adequate help in terms of casework, by the:

> formation and execution of a plan which enlists on its side the mind of the distressed person, and gradually evokes and restores in him that capacity for control of circumstances.[48]

The emphasis on the dual aspects of prevention and cure contained in the idea of public assistance and casework charity prompted Bosanquet to remark that the difference between the reports was:

> that the preventive system of the Majority, while covering all the details which the other suggest [sic], is also so adjusted and adapted as to appeal to a preventive force which the Minority have not contemplated at all.[49]

Bosanquet believed that if the Minority wished to speak of the causes of poverty, it ought not to restrict itself to general preconditions, as in the case of sickness or unemployment. In some instances it might be perfectly correct, but in others, events like unemployment were effects rather than causes. It was the mind and will which was the real source of poverty. All action passed through the mediation of mind, a fundamental truth which, Bosanquet claimed, the Minority overlooked.

Environmental Factors

The Webbs had a very different view of the matter. They felt that both reports had totally destroyed the principles of the 1834 Poor Law, which they believed had been at the centre of COS theory. Sidney Webb saw the 1834 principles as resting on an atomic view of society, which he envisaged as being superseded by the more responsible and collectivist view of the state and the individual. Webb continued his argument with the accusation of overlapping implicit in the Majority Report, although this was, as I have suggested, an ambiguous point. Essentially Webb's argument, in his 1909 reply to Bosanquet, 'The end of the poor law' revolved on two main propositions.[50] First, the COS and the Majority wanted to pulverise the poor law and to substitute for it a new system. Webb took this proposition as a rod to beat the COS for ever having supported the poor law, to show that their timid proposals contradicted the evidence, and to castigate them for holding onto outdated ideas. The second proposition maintained that the COS and the Majority wanted to humanise, widen, and strengthen the poor law, or in other words, to make it function more efficiently. Webb took this proposition to show the COS and Majority ignorance of the decline of the poor law over the nineteenth century, and the gradual growth of state intervention, which had led to considerable overlapping in the provision of social services. It is obvious that both propositions are contradictory, but the question remains, did the Majority adhere to both? As the Webbs remarked elsewhere: 'The whole wording of the lengthy document [the Majority Report] points in one direction, and nearly all its definite proposals in another'.[51] The presupposition of this idea was that there was a radical difference between the old and new ideas about poverty. One of the ideas which the Webbs wanted to relate back to 1834 was that of defects in the citizen-mind. The Webbs in fact preferred to call it the 'moral factor in destitution', which Beatrice Webb mischievously described as one of those 'abstract controversies, which delighted the early Victorians'.[52]

In fact this early Victorian controversy was taken more seriously by the Webbs in an appendix to their *English Poor Law Policy*. The notion of moral defect was associated by the Minority Report with the stigma of pauperism and deterrence. Yet it also saw this position as 'the only philosophical argument that we have encountered'.[53]The Minority Report went on to refute this argument by asking: do the children, disabled, aged, and feeble-minded all suffer from defects in citizen-character? It raised the same question about the unemployed. The conclusion, apart from the familiar criticism of overlapping in the Majority Report, was that although 'individuals in all sections of the destitute may be morally defective, and this in all sorts of different ways, the great mass of destitution is the direct and ... almost inevitable result of the environment'.[54]

Although Beatrice Webb had commented on the Majority Report that 'what ... is clear, is that the COS party are desperately anxious to slur over everything which distinguishes one destitute person from another',[55] she and her husband could write that 'it is in the fullest sense true that the "moral factor" is the supreme issue'.[56] Later in the same essay they argued that it is the 'dominant consideration in every attempt at social reconstruction'.[57] Their argument here, however, was that the true foundation to individual character demanded a positive policy of state prevention. The moral factor was not an excuse for state inactivity but laid a positive duty on the state to intervene to prevent destitution. Without this policy the state was failing in its moral duty. In one sense the Webbs were not quite fair to the COS. They expressed an attitude which was neatly summarised by J.A. Hobson when he stated that 'the Charity Organisation philosophy, crystallised in the single phrase "in social reform character is the condition of conditions", represents a mischievous half-truth, the other half of which rests in the possession of the less thoughtful section of the social democrats'.[58] But it is clear that the COS did want to see those in temporary difficulty, the sick, and the feeble-minded treated differently from each other. As argued earlier, they had pioneered much of the separate treatment. In reply to Hobson's criticisms, the Bosanquets pointed out that the COS believed in positive help, with medical treatment, convalescence, training and retraining.[59] Many other individuals, however, needed detailed casework, and this was the area in which character was at issue. The Webbs also recognised the importance of the 'moral factor' as part of their philosophy of the minimum. As J.H. Muirhead pointed out in his account of the two reports, *By What Authority*, it was no part of a true collectivism to neglect the role of character.[60] Yet the question remains—what did this moral factor of 'character' imply? Both reports recognise its role. Were the Webbs, in holding onto the idea, harping back to the 1834 Poor Law? Were the COS, in looking to an alteration of the poor law and recognising the key role of the environment in creating much of the destitution they wished to treat, forward looking?

The ambiguity of 'character' can be illustrated by examining the COS arguments. The character of an individual has a determinate effect on his or her activity and circumstances. The COS sometimes called this the individual's 'standard of life', which is essentially that level of existence acceptable to the person. This connects with Helen Bosanquet's argument about the interests of the person. The standard of life is not a purely material standard, although it is not unrelated to material issues. As Helen Bosanquet pointed out, 'wages alone ... cannot put good things into a man's life; but it is none the less true that without good wages he cannot avail himself of them to the fullest extent'.[61] The COS were in fact progressively pushed by the logic of their argument on the standard of life to accept certain state-guaranteed levels. Total independence and total dependence were equally illusions. Each person began life as a socially dependent being. Through childhood and youth there was a necessary reliance upon the guidance of institutions. The conscious concern with the individual showed itself in a particular emphasis on the individual's role, which was bound up with ideas of character, will, interest, and mind. The characteristic Idealist principle was that the good of the state lay in the good will of those comprising it. This good will needed some degree of social maintenance to function. It needed guidance till maturity, then training and education. Although the COS admitted the need for individual responsibility and thrift, they still recognised the key role of centralised official bodies that would cultivate the good will and character of individual citizens. Their position entailed a far more strict and prescriptive form of social guidance than has usually been associated with the COS.

The caricatured view of the COS and the Majority is that they wanted self-help to flourish and individuals to take full responsibility for their actions. But the COS also believed in some form of equality of opportunity, in the sense that people should equally possess the chance to be responsible and to improve themselves. As the equality of opportunity argument implied, certain guaranteed levels of welfare provision would be necessary. Thus the COS notion of individual responsibility was only partial, as was also evident in the COS vocabulary of deserving and undeserving, or wilful incapacity and unwilled incapacity. In fact this distinction fails to catch the full meaning of the COS argument, which maintained that, even in the case of wilful incapacity, the individual was not totally responsible. As the COS recognised, the family environment often had a lot to do with the failure of one of its members. Poverty was essentially a reflection of the capacities of mind and character in the material circumstances of the individual. Yet the pursuit of good character could presuppose wide-ranging, centralised, official intervention.[62] In its concern for adequate pensions, hospitals, asylums, convalescent homes, housing, sanitation, and the like, the COS admitted the key role of the environment in relation to certain categories of destitution. Self-help was therefore viewed in the context of

parameters defined by organised casework and the state. As
Helen Bosanquet argued:

> It is one of the stock accusations against the society that it is blindly
> opposed to all intervention of the state on behalf of the poor; but in
> reviewing its history we are amazed to find how constantly the
> accusation is refuted.[63]

She goes on to cite examples of housing and sanitary work
sponsored by the COS.

A Question of Emphasis

Throughout the early 1900s, an increasing self-consciousness
about principles, arguments, and social change developed in the
COS, which was reflected in the Majority Report. That Report
encapsulated many of the tensions within the theories of the
society and in one sense brought them to a head. The extremely
critical attitude to the 1834 Poor Law, the intrinsic flexibility of
the public assistance committee proposal, and the greater
readiness to accept state activity on problems like unemployment, caused some heart searching in the society. Probably the
COS did not come to an equilibrium till it changed its name to
the Family Welfare Association, and, of course, accepted the
Beveridge Report in the 1940s.

One of the problems in dealing with the Majority proposals
arises from the transitional nature of the COS. Their ideas
underwent a series of slow, almost imperceptible changes
between 1870 and 1909. It is my contention that these changes
arose from the very logic of the COS arguments. The process
caused considerable tensions within the society and also in the
attitudes of historians to the society. Many social historians have
found it difficult to deal with the COS objectively. For example,
in T.H. Marshall's view it was 'repugnant to the modern mind'.[64]
The COS was, in fact, disliked both by the older philanthropists
and by the new collectivists. It represented a transition between
welfare as an indiscriminate gift of charity and as a right. It
established the principles of a right to receive help and of the
duty of all citizens to help. This help, its adherents argued, must
be consistently and systematically organised and should no
longer rely on occasional sympathy but on a positive voluntary
rational response, a response which at times could be exercised
by the state. Since the heyday of the COS, many of the types of
social work and charity it practised have been taken over by the

state in terms of statutory obligations. Yet many of the areas of
state involvement and non-involvement have been hotly disputed
in this century. The COS arguments have been central to the
continuing debate on the limits of state action and the extent of
individual freedom. Perhaps the COS is still too near in time to
be dealt with historically in a wholly objective manner.

One of the main reasons for internal tension in the COS was
not in fact due to its adherence to anachronistic Victorian social
theory, but rather to its conception of casework. Casework
encapsulated the wider COS view of social work, which, as we
have seen, was based upon an oscillating, ambiguous principle
of individual responsibility. As presented by Loch and the
Bosanquets, casework implied that economic matters were not
the sole problem of social work. Economic hardship and the
material environment were facets of a total problem; the individuals, their families, and specifically their minds and consciousness interacted in complex ways with economic, environmental,
and medical problems. The COS idea of casework assumed that
mind *per se* was created and structured within an environment
which played a key role in the formation of attitudes and
interests. The COS arguments about casework qualified the
Idealist theory of mind dominating the environment. The COS
were pushed into admitting more and more environmental
influences on the individual, especially through the principle of
partial responsibility, although in admitting these influences they
did not abandon the principles of mind and character.

The COS were thus caught in a dilemma. They recognized what
the Webbs saw as the old idea of character and the moral factor
in destitution, yet they also recognised what the Webbs regarded
as the modern idea, namely the environmental root to much
poverty and the necessary role of the state in eradicating it. The
COS had in fact been circling the problem throughout the 1890s
and the 1900s. The central question at issue for it was how far
should an individual be allowed to decline before the state or
some official body intervened, and how far was this intervention
compatible with the individual's self-development, character, and
freedom? In this sense Sidney Webb was probably correct in his
estimation of the Majority Report. Consciously or not, the COS
were affirming two contradictory propositions, or at least
apparently contradictory ones. In fact it is arguable that the COS
were aiming at some kind of synthesis, which would have been

more in tune with the actual spirit of the time than were the
Webbs' ideas. The Majority Report was basically confusing and
certainly not consistent, but in some respects it was only
reflecting the confusions of the wider society. This point possibly
helps to account for its greater public impact, a fact which seems
to have piqued the Webbs.

Although in appearance presenting a far more consistent
picture, the Webbs also saw the importance of individual choice,
character, and morality. Yet the impression is gained that they
never fully grasped the nettle. A revealing passage from Beatrice
Webb's diary hints at their real conception, where she states
that:

> we staked our hopes on the organised working class, served and
> guided, it is true, by an elite of unassuming experts who would make
> no claim to superior status, but would content themselves with
> exercising the power inherent in superior knowledge.[65]

The Webbs' superior knowledge, however unassuming, strode out
firmly on moral issues. As they laconically remarked:

> If families which prefer dirt, disorder and disease are to be forced by
> persistent pressure to mend their ways, what a terrible restriction on
> the liberty of the individual.[66]

In a similar vein they recommended the 'systematic enforcement
of parental responsibility'.[67] Like the COS, the Webbs had no
sympathy for the workshy and lazy. They also recommended
detention colonies for this residual group. And they placed great
emphasis on the enforced minimum, in order to 'clean up' the
base of society. The individual's work, home, parental responsibility, wages, and presumably procreation, would all be part of
the enforced minimum, and would also be part of what the
unassuming élite of natural superiors would deal with. As one
critic has remarked, 'the Webbs, who after all were the Minority
Report, preferred to emphasise the duties of citizenship and had
no confidence in actual citizens'.[68] Ample evidence for this
assertion can be found throughout the Webb's work.

Aware of the problems of the environment, the COS and the
Majority wanted to have confidence in the rights and duties of an
independent citizen body. In so doing they fell into contradic-
tions, a fact easily exploited by their critics. This is not to argue
for any crude conclusion regarding the rightness of either report.
It seems necessary, however, to qualify any judgement regarding

the predominance of the Minority in historical writings. In fact the two reports represent mere differences of emphasis on the same point about the causes of poverty. On many questions, the Majority, although less settled and clear cut than the Minority, demonstrates more adequately the intrinsic difficulties and anxieties felt by many at that time regarding the nature of reform and poverty. Many of these difficulties can be seen in the very logic of the arguments used by Bosanquet and Loch.

Conclusion

This essay is not an apologia for the COS or the Majority Report; rather it is an appeal for a better understanding of the arguments involved. In this sense it is also an attempt to demythologise certain views. The COS were not, in the 1900s, advocates of individualism in any direct, simple sense. The ideas behind the Majority Report, and those presented by Loch and the Bosan-quets, were bound up with an ethical individualism structured through the doctrines of philosophical Idealism. The Majority Report has been markedly misunderstood on this point. The COS itself was essentially a transitional organisation which reflected many implicit tensions on the issue of poverty. Its members were not simply anti-statists. This might seem an extremely odd judgement of Bernard Bosanquet, the author of *The Philosophical Theory of the State*. The ideas expressed by Bosanquet and Loch were underpinned by a complex social theory, again related to Idealist theory. In contrast, the Minority Report was not really so forward looking a document as its admirers have claimed. It reflected, indeed, the less congenial side of the Webbs' thought: their incurable partiality for élites and for bureaucratic organis-ation.

The Working Class and State 'Welfare' in Britain, 1880-1914

Pat Thane

The Middle Class and the Welfare State

SOME years ago Henry Pelling offered one of his stimulating and provocative challenges to the conventional wisdom of labour history. He pointed out that it is often assumed that the significant extensions of the welfare activities of the state by the post-1906 Liberal governments were in some way associated with the growth of the organised labour movement; that they were, if not simply responses to pressure from Labour (which has rarely been seriously argued), at least supported and welcomed by a significant proportion of the working class, and therefore could be expected by Liberal politicians to increase their credit with working-class voters, perhaps sufficiently to persuade them to resist the lure of Labour.

Pelling argued that this assumption was incorrect, that the mass of working people were hostile or indifferent to state welfare at least until *after* measures such as old-age pensions and national insurance were introduced; that Labour and socialist politicians who proposed welfare reforms, such as the Webbs or Hyndman, were themselves middle class. Working-class dislike of state welfare, he suggested, derived partly from a deeply rooted preference for independence and self-help, partly from suspicion of the state as a complex of institutions run by or on behalf of the rich (as apparently exemplified by the constraints imposed by the courts upon trade union activity, culminating with Taff Vale); and partly from experience of state social intervention which was seen rather rarely to have brought unmixed benefit to workers. He instanced popular hatred of the poor law, of compulsory

This chapter first appeared as an article in *The Historical Journal*, Vol. 27, No. 4, 1984, pp. 877-900 and is reproduced here by permission.

education, which deprived poor families of the vital earnings of their children, and of local authority housing and clearance policies which appeared to dis-house as many as were housed. He added that there is no evidence that social policy issues influenced working-class voters in national elections. He concluded that the Liberal reforms came about largely due to middle-class pressure and because Liberal politicians, notably Asquith, Lloyd George and Churchill, 'thought them desirable' and were able to finance them. He did not explore why they thought them desirable, though he rather dismissed the possibility that they consciously sought to prevent the loss of working-class votes to Labour.[1]

If Pelling was correct, he offered an important pointer to working-class political attitudes and expectations before 1914 and he opened up new questions: how, and why, did official Labour and working-class attitudes so change in the succeeding generation that by 1945 Labour was popularly identified as the party of social reform and became the party which created the modern 'welfare state'?

The Mistrust of State Welfare

There is considerable evidence to support Pelling's contentions, stronger sometimes than he was himself able to offer, since he actually provides rather little. Evidence from voting in national elections is not a sure guide to attitudes to specific issues, since votes were determined by a variety of pressures and issues, among which social legislation was not the most prominent in elections between the 1880s and 1914; and many of the poor had no vote. The scattered evidence from local elections (for school boards and boards of poor law guardians as well as for the local councils) which more frequently turned upon social issues, rather supports his view, since turn-out was usually low even after the local franchise changes in 1894 which enabled most workers to vote and to stand for election at the local level.

The difficulties of establishing the attitudes of the heterogeneous working class by other means are obvious. The surviving expressions of contemporary opinion are generally those of working-class organisations which, as Pelling has so often reminded us, were institutions often with middle- or lower middle-class leadership and composed of the better paid, more secure workers. The need of such workers for 'welfare' was, if not necessarily less than that of the very poor, often different in kind. Members of trade unions, friendly societies, co-operative and political organisations were, nevertheless, workers; and organisations generally exercise more influence in society than isolated individuals. Hence it is worth, as a first step, trying to establish their views.

To some degree, these support Pellings' contentions, though for reasons which he did not explore in depth. The largest exclusively working-class organisations of the period were the friendly societies, which had about 5.6 million members in Great Britain in 1900, when trade union members totalled about 1.2 million. They were run democratically by and for better paid, regularly employed manual workers, though they included many low-paid but regularly employed agricultural workers. As institutions centrally concerned with mutual insurance against sickness and old age, they had an especial interest in proposals for state-provided social security.[2] The largest of them was the Manchester Unity of Oddfellows (713,000 members in 1899). State provision, especially of old-age pensions, was frequently discussed at regular local and national meetings and in the Unity's journal between the early 1880s and 1914. The dominant though not universal view expressed was, in conformity with Pelling's expectations, that self-help was morally and socially preferable to redistributive provision implemented by a state which many members thought was increasingly and excessively powerful and intrusive.[3] This view was also strongly expressed in many smaller societies, other than the temperance institutions which saw drink as the major obstacle to the moral and material advance of the masses.[4] (The third largest society was the temperance society, the Order of Rechabites.)

There were however other views in the friendly societies. One, of growing influence, simply favoured state social reform, on the grounds that many were in need and only the state had the resources to help them in the short run; the state, furthermore, had a duty to support those who worked to sustain it. Its supporters advocated new taxes, in particular a land tax and a graduated income tax, to be earmarked for financing reform.[5]

The second largest society, the Ancient Order of Foresters (AOF: 666,000 members in 1899) also debated the issue at a variety of levels, especially in relation to old-age pensions. In general, the Foresters opposed state welfare, at least until around 1904. But the grounds most frequently expressed (most explicitly in the editorials of their monthly periodical, *Foresters' Miscellany*) were not the familiar orthodoxy of self-help, nor even, as has been suggested, self-preservation. Rather, it was repeatedly urged that the reform proposals of the politicians should be treated with suspicion, for they were means of evading the just demands of the working class for higher wages and regular work. They and the employers supported social reform because it was cheaper than increasing wages, the more so because 'welfare' would be paid for by the working class themselves. The latter, it was argued, were the main contributors to central government revenue, from which reform was expected to be financed; more revenue was derived from indirect taxes on tea, tobacco, alcohol and cocoa, which were paid disproportionately by the working class, than from the income tax and death duties levied on the wealthy. If the state were to implement new social legislation the Foresters would have preferred it to be financed by local rates which, at least in theory, were progressive taxes levied according to the value of property.[6]

But members were urged to oppose pensions and other state welfare measures and instead to support trade unions in the struggle for higher wages. The success of this struggle, it was argued, would enable workers to save for periods of sickness and old age and for other needs. In this way, they would retain their independence, which was preferable to increasing dependence upon, and control by, a state which operated in the interests of an opposing class; for, the journal argued:

> thinking men will fail to see why capitalists should be relieved of their duty of contributing to the maintenance of many persons whose very poverty was caused by capitalists' appropriation of a very large measure of the fruits arising from the labour of those poor people who have to seek the aid of the rates in old age.[7] ...If a workman attends as diligently to his work as does his capitalist employer, why on earth should he not be made to rely on his wage to meet all his requirements as well as the employer depends upon his profits to meet all his requirements?[8] ...The aim of the working class ought to be to bring about economic conditions in which there should be no need for distribution of state alms. The establishment of a great scheme of state pensions would legalize and stamp as a permanent feature of our social life the chronic poverty of the age. The desire of the best reformers is to remove the conditions that make that poverty, so that every citizen shall have a fair chance not only of earning a decent wage for today but

such a wage as shall enable him to provide for the future.[9] ...Employers have presented carefully organized barriers to the workmen getting more wages.[10] ...Man is a responsible being. To rob him of his responsibility is to degrade him. The working class should rise to the occasion and insist upon being capable of using their own wages to their own advantage.[11]

Furthermore, *Foresters' Miscellany* argued, collective action could help the impoverished masses outside the friendly society movement. Towards this group, contrary to a frequent interpretation of friendly society attitudes,[12] the Foresters expressed a particular responsibility as fellow members of the working class. They recognised that their wages and conditions of work currently made it impossible for them to save systematically,[13] but urged that the solution lay not in further exhortations to unattainable self-help or through state handouts, but through regular work and higher wages, which might be achieved through collective working-class pressure.

The AOF was, like all friendly societies, an explicitly non-political organisation, though the editor of its journal had obviously absorbed some of the language and concepts of socialism. The peak of his exhortations coincided with and reflected the spurt of trade union growth and activity in the 1880s. His arguments seem to have been acceptable to the mass of membership. They suggest that some at least of the working class opposed state welfare for reasons rooted in a collectivist rather than an individualist conception of working-class independence and mutual support, and in a clear, but not necessarily revolutionary, conception of the opposition of interests between classes.

'Reform' Perceived as a Capitalist Tool

If the friendly societies exhibited a variety of attitudes towards state welfare, so too did the labour movement as more conventionally defined. The Social Democratic Federation was not the most influential sector of this movement, but its attitudes to state welfare were especially fully developed. They deserve some attention because they represent a persistent though minority strand in working-class thinking, and the debate in the SDF influenced individuals who were active in the public debate on welfare; for example Will Crooks and other members of the Poplar board of guardians in east London who sought to implement progressive policies from the mid-1890s.[14]

The central problem for a revolutionary party like the SDF in this context was whether social reform from a capitalist state could advance the prospects for socialism or hold it back. Three things have to be emphasised in the background to this debate: first, that many in the SDF recognised that Britain in the 1880s, 1890s and 1900s was not in a revolutionary situation; second, that concrete proposals for state welfare reforms were being made and looked increasingly as if they might be implemented by politicians who were distinctly not socialist, indeed, were explicitly anti-socialist.[15] Joseph Chamberlain, for example, recognised more shrewdly than any other politician the potential of social reform to preserve and even strengthen the existing political and economic order. From the late 1880s he advocated state old-age pensions and improved working-class housing, with a shorter working day and minimum wages among other things, not only because they were desirable in themselves, as he believed, but also because they could ensure social and political stability and diminish the influence of Labour. In the 1890s he advocated redistributive welfare on the grounds that 'the foundations of property are made more secure when no real grievance is felt by the poor against the rich'.[16]

The third important influence on deliberations in the SDF was the assumption that most of the poorer working class wanted social reform and would accept it in any form other than the poor law; that though workers might criticise specific reforms where, as in the case of compulsory education, they brought them no clear material gain, they did not oppose them in principle; that they had more hope of necessary material improvement through reform from the existing state than from the uncertain prospect of a transition to socialism. Hence the immediate problem posed for revolutionaries was how were they, in a situation not particularly favourable to them, to prevent the working class falling into Chamberlain's trap?

The answer of William Morris and the Socialist League in the 1880s was firmly that the capitalist state was incapable of conceding social reforms which benefited anyone but capitalists and was infinitely resistant to attempts to change it; state welfare could not benefit the working class until the working class had itself seized state power. There were supporters of this view in the SDF,[17] but the influential majority argued that outright opposition to state welfare would alienate working-class support and enhance the prospects for the success of Chamberlain's tactics. The revolutionary left had not the effective political power to prevent Liberals or Conservatives implementing reforms if they chose to do so—the more so since they could offer no immediate alternative. The distant prospect of revolution was unlikely to be more attractive to the poor than the tangible, if small, material improvements of a pension or a better house offered by the orthodox politicians.[18] Even if it had been less remote, few believed that revolution had mass appeal. J. Hunter-Watts gloomily wrote: 'We claim adult suffrage but we know if it were established tomorrow and a vote taken whether all prominent socialists should be hanged, a majority might send us to the gallows'.[19] And, in all humanity, revolutionaries found it hard to oppose real material gains for the desperately poor when they could offer no plausible substitute.

Yet most SDF activists firmly believed that state social reforms were an important part of the capitalist strategy to defeat social- ism and keep the working class in subjection. Proposals, they argued, such as a 5s. old-age pension would only marginally improve the material conditions of the poor and would not change the situation which made that condition possible. Rather they would enable workers to reach accommodation with a situation in which employers paid inadequate wages in insecure conditions of employment. Reform was built into the capitalist system, was among the mechanisms for making capitalism plausible among those who gained least from it; it was part of the classic strategy for avoiding confrontation and revolution. Recognising all of this seemed to put the SDF in a particularly difficult dilemma: they could neither effectively oppose nor conscientiously support apparently popular current proposals.

An influential majority of them, however, argued that the choice was not quite so stark as this. A qualified critical acceptance of some social reform was an entirely respectable socialist strategy. Theoretically it was possible to build within the capitalist system alternative institutions with an alternative socialist content that ultimately would force capitalism to a crisis. This was the theoretical basis of the SDF's approach to social reform from the late 1880s, most articulately expressed by J. Hunter Watts and Harry Quelch.[20] It was strengthened by the belief that but for the existence of an increasingly organised and articulate working- class movement, the capitalist parties would not by the 1880s and 1890s have been brought to the point of out-manoeuvring socialism by offering social reform. Hence the SDF's adoption of a reform strategy—'stepping stones to socialism' as Hyndman called it. This did not imply supporting Chamberlain's reforms, or any others which could not be seen to be predominantly in the working-class interest. Instead they tried to distinguish between reforms which were mere 'sops', and those which could make inroads into the basis of capitalism, which redistributed wealth and so improved the material conditions of the working class that they could become stronger and more active in the class struggle.[21]

Hence the programme of the SDF from its foundation committed it to 'measures to palliate the evils of our existing society': artisan housing at low rents, free compulsory education, school meals, the eight-hour day, graduated tax on incomes above £300 p.a., nationalisation of railways, banks and land, co-operative organisation of agriculture under state direction.[22] The problem remained, of course, for revolutionaries that though these reforms, if implemented, *might* strengthen the revolutionary potential of the working class, there was at least as likely a chance that even these would strengthen capitalism by making workers complacent and unwilling to struggle for further change.[23]

The SDF aimed to counter this possibility partly by propaganda, designed to educate workers into awareness of the *real* aims of capitalist reform, but also through an emphasis upon reform at the municipal level, beginning, Hyndman hoped, with a 'Commune for London'.[24] They wished to get socialists elected to local councils, boards of poor law guardians, and school boards, where they could hope to influence the administration of policy and to improve working-class conditions. They could also encourage the taking into municipal ownership of major utilities such as gas and water supply and, in the long run, enterprises of all kinds; and the improvement of working conditions and wages for municipal employees. Increased working-class participation in local government, the SDF believed, would strengthen their awareness of their potential power; socialist-controlled municipalities would provide living examples of the socialist alternative within capitalist society, as well as providing admirable practical experience of administration for revolutionaries. But also and equally important, they would provide a permanent check on the growth of central bureaucracy which they identified as one of the most dangerous tendencies in nineteenth-century society, strengthening the control of the state over the lives of individuals and increasing the enslavement of the masses. For revolutionaries the growth of the capitalist state was a particular and immediate danger. The more it grew, the harder it was to overthrow. But Hyndman and many others in the pages of *Justice* (the journal of the SDF) saw centralised bureaucracy as equally dangerous and equally likely in socialist society. In their view the municipalities should be *permanent* alternative sources of power, permanent checks on the centralising, enslaving state.[25]

Support for municipalisation had the further merit for the SDF of wide potential appeal in a society in which suspicion of centralisation was considerably stronger than support for the SDF's version of socialism. They shared with the Foresters the suspicion that the purpose and likely outcome of current reform proposals was at least as much to undermine the collective and individual independence of the masses as to improve their material condition. However, whereas the Foresters looked to trade union action as the alternative strategy for achieving social progress and rejected state welfare, the SDF, always hostile to the unions, looked to political action and a strategy of encouraging certain forms of state welfare.

The question of whether material improvement for the working class was best attained by industrial or political action or by a combination of both was central to the welfare debate in the working-class movement and was obviously of especial salience within the trade unions. Trade union attitudes, predictably, varied: over time, partly in accordance with their level of strength; among different occupational groups; and between leaders and rank and file. They were influenced also by the degree to which welfare was involved in industrial bargaining and in management. Many workers—probably increasing numbers in the 1890s—experienced employers' use of company welfare schemes to counter demands for higher wages, to reduce turnover among essential workers, and to diminish the appeal of the trade unions' own benefits.[26] This heightened suspicions of the purposes of welfare. Equally important was the experience of administering benefits, which were an important means of attracting and holding members. They served also to reinforce the ethic of mutual support. Similarly, benefit regulations reflected and reinforced working people's own definitions of the boundary between 'deserving' and 'undeserving' poverty: unions would give benefits to strikers, to the unjustly dismissed or to those forced temporarily to leave their trade to take lower-status labouring work, but not to drunkards, malingerers or petty criminals.[27] Friendly society benefits followed similar norms: claims were investigated by members to ensure that disreputable 'brothers' were not betraying the trust and hard-earned contributions of their fellow workers.[28] Such rules should not necessarily be seen as evidence of working-class internalisation of the values of individualistic self-help so tirelessly preached to them by their 'betters'—though many working people *did* internalise them, however inappropriately. Such values as hard work, sobriety, discipline, loyalty and respect for the sacrifices of fellow workers were as essential to a successful workers' movement as to successful capitalism.

Against this background social reform issues were widely debated in the trade union movement. Questions of subsidised working-class housing, free education to university level, state medical services and old-age pensions were regularly debated at TUC conferences from the early 1890s, and won majority support. The increased trade union interest in welfare issues at this time may have arisen because they were of more immediate political importance in the 1890s when politicians were putting forward serious proposals. It may also be due to the increased influence in the TUC in the 1890s of representatives of the general unions. Not only did these unions represent workers for whom destitution was a more probable contingency than it was for the craftsmen of the older unions, but the unions were initially less likely to provide 'friendly' benefits for their members than were the older unions, or, if they did provide them, to do so at lower levels. The 'new' unionists argued in the 1890s not only that their members could not afford the higher subscriptions necessary for the provision of benefits, but that such activities were diversions from the central objectives of unions, which were the attainment of improved wages and working conditions. They argued that the need to preserve sufficient funds to meet benefit obligations might inhibit unions from undertaking costly industrial action.[29] Nevertheless, their members urgently needed greater security in times of sickness, unemployment or old age, and proposed provision for them by the state or other means was of major interest to their leaders. The most desirable forms of provision were not so easy to define or to agree upon.

Numbers of both liberal and socialist trade unionists argued that rather than pursue social reforms the unions should direct their energies to improving wages and conditions of employment and to achieving full employment, so that working people could maintain their independence of the centralising state and, undivided and strengthened by this struggle, carry on fighting for further working-class gains.[30] Many recognised the danger that 'welfare' benefits would enable employers to continue paying inadequate wages and could make working people complacent and unwilling to organise.[31] They also recognised that the very poor had every reason for reluctance to await the outcome of long-term strategies. However, they placed their faith in the success of the 'right to work' campaigns of the 1890s and after, and in increasing working-class representation in local and central government. Many trade unionists saw the industrial and parliamentary roads as complementary rather than competing routes to a regenerated society in which state welfare would be required only as a safety net beneath the provision workers could make for themselves and for one another. Meanwhile there was little faith that the major political parties would provide any real benefit for workers and general criticism of the inadequacy of their reform proposals.[32] As the *Cotton Factory Times* put it in 1890:

> We plainly confess that we are anything but enamoured of this growing tendency to enact laws governing the private concerns of workmen. It may be an open question as to whether our houses should be built and our hours of labour regulated by the state, but we must have our eyes open to where it is leading us to. The people who have much done for them gradually lose their backbone just as muscles which are not used become weak and flabby. The result is that the habit of leaning on a support grows stronger until in time there will be no individual strength left. We sincerely believe that is what the German Emperor is aiming at. When people look to the state and receive from it almost everything they get, they will become the strongest supporters of those from whom they obtain their privileges. But they may rest assured that they who pull the wires will take care that in exchange for this the puppet shall not dance to a tune of its own calling. The grip of the state will be gradually tightened until it will be almost impossible for a man to speak except in regulation tones. A people under the heel of such a tyranny cannot in the battle of life be permanently prosperous. If

workmen want to insure let them do it themselves. If they wish to provide for their old age, the proper course is to save part of their wages ... The workman's duty is to combine and see to it that he gets his full share of the produce of his labour, and let him do his own saving if he wishes. This system has developed the finest and freest people the world has produced, and has placed them at the head of the industrial peoples of the earth.[33]

But if this expressed a widespread view among union leaders, rank-and-file spinners, experiencing low pay, poor housing and no dramatic gains from years of trade union organisation, were unimpressed by such high-minded abstractions and were more willing to place their faith in action by the state or the local authority than in hypothetical long-term gains by the trade union movement.[34]

There is a need for more systematic examination of trade union attitudes, in view of their extreme variety.[35] Pelling is however likely to be mistaken in suggesting that 'on questions of social reform ... the leaders of the unions and the politicians of the Labour party ... were in fact more progressive than their rank-and-file'. He defines 'progressive' as implying support for state social reforms and, as we have seen, it could be more 'progressive' and 'radical' to oppose social reforms, from a socialist standpoint, than to support them; and such divisions of opinion do not appear to correspond with any clear horizontal division within the unions.[36]

The Trades Councils and Political Activism

Radical opposition to proposed reforms was also evident among trades councils. Throughout the 1890s and 1900s, trades councils in large and small towns throughout the country devoted a large proportion of their time to discussion, investigation and agitation about the need for more and better working-class housing, old-age pensions, working-class education at all levels, health care, school meals, poor law reform, against sweated labour, for railway nationalisation and cheap fares, even in one case for more consideration of the problem of 'unmarried wives'. Most favoured extended municipalisation. After 1892 they directed their energies towards the election and co-option of their members to local councils, boards of poor law guardians and boards of education, with some success, often insisting that their members report back regularly on the activities of the bodies on which they sat.

Trades councils surveyed local needs, particularly of housing and employment. They initiated working-class tours of municipal institutions such as workhouses, poor law infirmaries, schools and waterworks, arguing vigorously that ratepayers had a right to inspect and evaluate institutions which they financed. They published their findings and took up workers' complaints against publicly and philanthropically funded establishments. The most energetic councils, such as Bradford, issued pamphlets inform-ing workers of their rights in the administration of the poor law and workmen's compensation.[37]

This high level of interest and activity appears to have been stimulated both by the changing position of the trades councils in the 1890s, as more socialists entered them and pressure for labour representation increased, leading some Liberals to disengage themselves from their activities; and by the legislation of the early 1890s, which permitted more working-class involve-ment in local elected bodies, and implemented such reforms as the Housing of the Working Classes Act, 1890.[38]

But the councils were not generally uncritical in welcoming these measures as symptoms of social progress, though some of their members were inclined to be so; rather, they believed in their extreme inadequacy. Like other groups they went through a process of debate about the terms on which they should accept state 'welfare'. Many of them shared the acute doubts and dilemmas apparent elsewhere among socialists and working-class groups, as, for example, in 1894 when Liverpool Trades Council was invited to join a local committee, under the chair-manship of W.H. Lever, to explore ways to diminish the high rate of unemployment in the city. Many members opposed this class collaboration in philanthropy:

> Most of the council didn't like it at all ... but when we saw the starva-tion and misery existing in our midst through lack of employment we considered it our duty to help and find some method of easing the suffering of our contemporaries.[39]

Many trades-council members experienced a similar conflict over collaboration with state welfare measures which they believed might not be in the best long-term interests of their class, but which alleviated short-term need. The way out of this dilemma for many of them lay in increasing belief in the possib-ility of effecting working-class representation in local and national politics. Whilst not necessarily optimistic about the degree of change which could be achieved by this means, they concluded that to maximise working-class influence upon the making and administration of local and central policy was the only realistic course open to them.[40]

A similar spirit lay behind the working-class pressure groups which sprang up in the 1890s, backed by trades councils, unions and political clubs. They included; the National Committee of Organized Labour for the Promotion of Old-Age Pensions For All (founded 1898), the Workmen's National Housing Council (founded 1898), and Anti-Sweating League (1898), the National Association for the Promotion of Workmen's Trains (1896) and the Railway Nationalization Society (1908).

The first of these grew out of the contemporary public debate about state pensions. Although initiated by a middle-class Congregationalist minister, F.H. Stead, and sustained by funds from Charles Booth and the Cadburys, it was kept in being until 1908 by the energy of Frederick Rogers, a self-educated book-binder, an active trade unionist and first secretary of the Labour Representation Committee. He was supported by a committee chaired by W.C. Steadman of the barge builders' union and consisting of trades council and friendly society representatives. It was a more 'working-class' body than Pelling suggests.[41] The committee's campaign for a non-contributory 5s. per week for all at 65 was waged through public meetings organised by local trades councils, pamphleteering and lobbying, steering always a non-sectarian course in the interests of gaining maximum support. Rogers was, in any case, no revolutionary; he had some success.[42] Pensions were probably the most popular state welfare proposal before 1908, but the popularity even of this cause ebbed and flowed. Rogers found it almost impossible to arouse enthusiasm or even interest during the Boer war.[43] In 1901 the Leicester Trades Council reported:

> ...general apathy ... it is not only the middle and upper classes who are indifferent but also the great masses of working men and women. We realize this bitterly enough in a working-class town like Leicester.[44]

Even in 1904 support and funds were so low that Rogers temporarily took another job.[45] Popular interest only revived with the approach of the General Election.

The Workmen's National Housing Council grew out of the concern with housing questions evident in working men's political clubs and in the SDF. Initiated by Fred Knee, another self-educated working man, a member both of the SDF and of the Fabian Society, the WNHC aimed to make housing a more prominent issue in the labour movement and to campaign against unjust eviction and for subsidised housing at low rents by persuading local authorities to implement their permissive powers under the 1890 Act.[46] Like the NCOL it operated through local committees based on trades councils employing conventional pressure group tactics. Again, W.C. Steadman was its president, but it had neither middle-class funding nor patronage. Forty trade union branches, trades councils and other working-class organisations were affiliated to it by 1906. Its main support and source of funding was the National Union of Operative Bricklayers.[47]

It had some success with the TUC. It worked in close association with the National Association for the Extension of Workmen's Trains which argued that more cheap fares would enable urban workers to take advantage of cheap suburban housing. Jointly they ran well-attended meetings at the opening of every TUC Conference from 1899 to 1913. But Knee believed that 'one man on a local body is worth 20 deputations'[48] and devoted especial attention to winning support on local councils, with some success among radical members of the LCC. During the 1900s the WNHC was especially critical of the LCC's much praised house-building programme for providing houses which were too small, at rents too high for those in greatest need.[49] The Council was convinced that only the state had sufficient resources to build the necessary homes and that it would employ them only when socialists influenced or controlled it.[50]

It was less confident of its popular appeal. Its monthly *Housing Journal* lamented in February 1901 that 'the mass of the working class as yet show no interest in the housing question. To arouse interest we must do more than pass resolutions'. Its attempts to stimulate more widespread militancy by encouraging rent strikes against private and local authority landlords had few successes. In Tottenham in 1901 the WNHC came 'very near to reaching our dream of some time since—a no-rent campaign'. Its members persuaded half the 353 private tenants on the Coleraine Park Estate to withhold rent, and achieved a reduction in a proposed rent increase from 1s. 6d to 6d per week. Elsewhere rent strikes aroused slight support.[51]

Such pressure groups were of marginal importance in the politics of the generation before 1914. They testify, however, to the existence of working-class support for state welfare—but for an alternative and more radical conception of its role than that of 'middle-class politicians'. They do not however demonstrate that their popular confidence in this alternative was very great.

'Reform' or Socialism?

More popular and more effective was the 'right to work' movement of the late 1890s and beyond. The large demonstrations of the unemployed, organised, in different parts of the country, by the SDF, by trades councils and by Independent Labour Party (ILP) branches, demanding public works and outdoor relief in the short run and an eight-hour day and a constructive government policy to deal with unemployment, led to more generous outdoor relief, public works and the establishment of labour bureaux in some localities and to the national Unemployed Workmen Act, 1905.[52]

On a broader range of issues, agitation for advanced reform was also led by the Women's Co-operative Guild, founded in 1884. The co-operative movement for much of this period was dominated by members determined to keep the movement apart from politics.[53] They stifled discussion of issues, such as social reform, which did not directly concern co-operative trading. But others strove to discuss political issues and insisted that, as a working-class organisation, the co-operative movement ought to take a stand upon them. Among the most articulate of these, particularly on reform issues, were the women of the guild, especially the impressive Margaret Llewellyn Davies, its first secretary, a woman of middle-class origins at the head of the largest female working-class organisation of the period. In a paper to the co-operative congress in 1890, she argued that working-class conditions could be materially and permanently improved through parliamentary action. The octogenarian George Holyoake replied: 'We desire to have the management of our own affairs. God has been very good to the rich, it remains for the co-operatives to be good to the poor by making, as it has the power to do, the fortune of labour. Within legitimate limits we shall avail ourselves of the help of parliament. We claim that the state should be impartial to us and remove any disability. We mean to make our own fortune by our own devices'[54]—a view of considerable influence in the co-operative movement.

Male members of the co-operative movement, if they were politically active, probably operated through other political organisations. It was perhaps the scarcity of other organisations for women that accounts for the high level of activity of the women of the guild: lobbying and demonstrating from the early 1890s to 1914 and beyond for better medical care for mothers and children, improved working-class housing, improved divorce legislation, against sweated labour, for a minimum wage, and old-age pensions, working with some success to get their members elected to school boards, boards of guardians, pension committees after 1908 and local insurance committees after 1911.[55]

Co-operative women, like the trades councils, organised working-class tours of rate-financed institutions to establish the right of ratepayers to keep watch upon their administration.[56] In the 1890s they tried persistently, though with no great success, to persuade respectable co-operators of their duty to extend their trading activities into poor districts and to adapt their practices to the needs of the poorest by lowering entrance fees and selling goods in small quantities. Margaret Llewellyn Davies shocked male members to the core by proposing—unsuccessfully—co-operative pawnshops, to provide a non-exploitative version of a necessary service for the very poor.[57]

The women of the guild accepted state social reform pragmatically as unavoidable, given the determination of especially the post-1906 Liberal government to provide it, and as conferring real and desirable, though generally inadequate, material benefits on the poor. They took it for granted that only the most persistent pressure on behalf of the working class would force a Conservative or Liberal government into real redistribution, and they played their part in exerting that pressure.

Awareness of the need for action to alleviate mass hardship, suspicion of the proposals of prominent politicians, and differences as to the desirable way forward were equally prominent in working-class political organisations. Such questions were widely discussed in local political clubs and in the ILP from its foundation.

Fears were, predictably, expressed that if the ILP were to channel too much energy into pressure for reforms, the movement would be diverted from the pursuit of 'socialism', rendering it indistinguishable from 'an advanced wing of liberalism', dedicated to creating 'a contented race of wage slaves'.[58] Since, however, many ILP supporters were *not* easily distinguishable from advanced liberals it is not surprising that this view vied with the belief that Labour should advocate, and would shortly be in a position to implement, radical reforms. From its formation, ILP leaders and publications criticised the limited reforms proposed by Chamberlain and others[59] and advocated: state-financed housing; free education to university level of a kind which would no longer merely fit the working class 'to be more highly productive wage slaves for the benefit of a possessing class';[60] free meals for schoolchildren; pensions for all at 60; labour exchanges; the 'right to work'; all to be financed through redistributive taxation.[61] Certain of these activities, they believed, would be most desirably initiated and financed at the local level. In the 1890s the ILP strenuously advocated municipal socialism rather than reform through the national state: 'since we believe that the smaller the unit of government the less likelihood is there of tyranny over the individual'.[62] Support for municipal socialism appears to have diminished in the 1900s as its limitations became apparent and Labour's success on the national level seemed a more realistic possibility.

The ILP put up candidates for local councils, boards of guardians and school boards, on programmes which included: improvement of the wages and work conditions of municipal employees; municipalisation of utilities; extension of public services and the administration of hospitals, schools and workhouses in what was perceived as the working-class interest. They had some limited and geographically uneven success.[63] The variety and implications of interest in municipal socialism in this period deserve more detailed attention than can be given here. But nowhere did working-class voters flood out to support such social reforming candidates, or indeed any others.

Within the ILP support for advanced reform generally did not conflict with firm convictions about the distinction between the helpable poor and the 'residuum'. The purpose of reform, as they saw it, was to give maximum aid to the majority of self-respecting, hard-working people whose wages and conditions of life kept them severely deprived despite their best efforts, and to do this in such a way as to support independence rather than to intrude upon people's lives or to encourage dependence upon and control by the state. Trade unions and political parties should, they thought, work together to this end.[64]

By the time of the general election of 1906, the political movement demonstrated a high degree of commitment to social reform. Labour Representative Committee election addresses in

1906, naturally, give greatest prominence to the principle of working-class representation and the repeal of Taff Vale, but 84 per cent of candidates mentioned unemployment as an issue, 81 per cent old-age pensions, 79 per cent education and 60 per cent housing; the assortment of SDF and other left-wingers gave similar prominence to these issues. By contrast, among Liberal candidates, 98 per cent of whom discussed the maintenance of free trade, and 86 per cent amendment of the controversial Conservative Education Act of 1902, only 69 per cent advocated pensions and poor law reforms, 41 per cent unemployment legislation and 36 per cent housing.[65]

Labour Reluctance, Liberal Reforms

There is some necessarily scattered and possibly unrepresentative evidence that 'advanced' state welfare had support among the unorganised, though responses predictably varied among different groups within the working class. Benefits which were unequivocal gains for better-off workers sometimes entailed sacrifices for the poorest which they understandably disliked. This was most obvious in the response to compulsory education. There can be no doubt about the widespread commitment among the organised working class to the expansion of educational opportunities at all levels.[66] But compulsory school education after 1880, though welcomed by many better-off workers, posed acute dilemmas for the very poor and for sympathetic radicals. It might increase the poverty of the poorest children by removing them from the employment market whilst offering their families no compensation, and indeed required them to pay fees until 1902, on the grounds that parents 'would rather be stimulated to a sense of duty and to a manly spirit of independence';[67] it understandably met uncertainty and even resistance during its first 20 years. In London in the 1890s poorer families resented compulsory attendance. Compulsion was widely evaded in poorer districts and intrusive attendance officers were sometimes physically attacked. However, by the 1900s after 20 years of legislative compulsion and especially after the abolition of elementary school fees in 1902, open opposition diminished, although truancy continued.[68] Compulsory education had placed poorer parents in a real dilemma as Annie Besant recognised from her experiences as a member of the London School Board in the 1890s; she met 'gaunt, hunger-pinched men and women

... decent folk who didn't want to keep their children ignorant, but sometimes there were no boots, sometimes there was a baby to feed, sometimes there was no food'.[69] F.J. Gould, the socialist and secularist, first a London school teacher, then member of the Leicester school board, after a conversation with a mother who kept her daughter at home to help with the house, commented in 1902 on:

> the painful complexity of interest involved—the mother's need of help; the child's need of education; society's claim that the child, as its ward, shall be trained in intelligent citizenship. The mother must yield; and the mother must suffer; but, alas, no commonwealth can truly gain by the suffering of mothers.[70]

But even those who could afford to sacrifice a child's wage might resent legal compulsion because it applied to working-class children in state elementary schools, but not to middle-class children; it seemed to assume the lesser capacity of the poor to make rational choices about their own lives.[71]

It is highly likely (as Pelling points out) that certain sections of the working class disliked certain measures: those who depended on their children's incomes might resent compulsory education, but might have welcomed it had their material circumstances been different; the inhabitants of the 'model tenements' built by the five-per-cent philanthropists often resented the close supervision of their behaviour, and complained of shoddy building and walls so thin that neighbours could not avoid overhearing each other's activities.[72] Reforms which required some sacrifice, such as education, were understandably less popular than those, such as pensions, which did not. Hence proposals for non-contributory pensions were more popular than for contributory.[73] Measures which entailed 'intrusion' into working-class lives and homes, and seemed to imply that poor people needed the guidance of their 'betters', were less popular than those which did not. There was resentment of the newly appointed health visitors at the turn of the century for inspecting working-class homes and child-rearing practices, and too often offering well-meaning advice which was simply inappropriate to the lives of the underpaid in miserable homes.[74] This is confirmed by R.H. Tawney's account of a conversation in 1912 with Edmund Hobson, a colliery weighman, and John Elkin, a miner, students of his at Longton:

> Myself: Any of you read *Seems So!*? Its main idea seems to be that working classes hate interference of rich—inspectors, visitors and so on in their affairs.

E. Hobson: Well they did hate the Health Visitors here at first, especially when they were single women. But they seem to welcome them now. It's a matter of habit. But the grievance is that the inspection and so on does not press upon everyone equally. No inspector thinks of going into houses in — Road. When I was at the elementary school the attendance officer would come round if I missed a day. When I went to the secondary school, no one bothered about it. People dislike that sort of interference because it's applied to one class and not another.

Elkin: It's the way in which they make us ignorant people live in the way they think we ought.[75]

The book to which Tawney referred, *Seems So! A Working Class View of Politics*, has been quoted as evidence of working-class opposition to interventionist state 'welfare'.[76] 'To the poor economic reform means a measure of justice between the "haves" and the "have-nots"; but social reform means "police" whether they are really required or not'.[77]

Seems So! repeatedly emphasises a growing working-class sense of alienation from politics, as supporting only the interests of another class which they had no actual or potential power to influence: 'As with football, the greater part of the players have become lookers-on, willing to cheer or jeer, but not to exert themselves'.[78] But this feeling that the working class could do little to change things was not inconsistent with continuing awareness and criticism of the operation of political processes and the class-biased nature of much state intervention and inspection. Above all, individuals resented the unwillingness of 'reformers' to treat working people with the respect and good fellowship of equals.

However, the writers of *Seems So!* defined as popularly acceptable 'economic' reforms which included the provision of working-class housing, legislation preventing food adulteration, and the Factory Acts. 'Social' reform, which they claimed was disliked, included the Children Act 1908 (which allowed inquiry into parents' care of their children and removal of the children if it was found wanting) and the temperance movement, because it passed judgements on individual leisure habits.[79] This was not the conventional distinction between 'economic' and 'social' and it does not suggest principled opposition to *all* conventionally defined social reform by the state. It suggests, again, opposition to state action or to private philanthropy which was inquisitorial, which sought to impose standards of behaviour upon the working class, and acceptance of reform which was non-punitive, redistributive and conferred real material improvement.

There is, of course, a major problem of the degree to which such pieces of evidence accurately reflect widespread working-class attitudes or are simply incidental illustrations. It is difficult in particular to know to what extent differences of local political culture created different attitudes. In parts of London, for example, where working-class organisation was relatively weak, optimism for social improvement by political means may have been less than in places like Bradford where it was strong. In the case of *Seems So!* it is often difficult to distinguish the personal comments of the middle-class writer Stephen Reynolds from those of his Devon fishermen collaborators, the Woolleys, despite Reynolds' insistence that the work was entirely collaborative.[80] But however they might differ in other respects, the distinction between inquisitorial, 'anti-working class', and redistributive reform was common to most of the groups and individuals discussed here. It certainly underlay the desire to participate in social policy making and administration at the local level.

Pelling suggests that welfare reforms became popular only *after* they were implemented by the post-1906 Liberal governments.[81] Some shifts of opinion or strategy did occur even before 1906. The National Conference of Friendly Societies resolved in 1904 to support non-contributory state pensions at 65, largely as a result of pressure from their own members and the manifest failure of alternative strategies to improve conditions for the aged poor over the preceding 15 years.[82] But further changes followed the general election of 1906, when the presence of a significant number of Labour members in parliament and a Liberal government prepared to implement actual reforms rather than just to talk about them, as had been the case for the previous 25 years, meant that the working-class movement had to define its attitude and act in response to *real* extensions of the reforming activity of the centralising state: the introduction of school meals and compulsory school medical inspection in 1906 and 1907; old-age pensions in 1908; labour exchanges and trade boards for the sweated trades in 1909; national health insurance and unemployment insurance in 1911; and the introduction of a graduated income tax after 1908.

The Liberal reforms and the presence of Labour in parliament intensified the previous splits of opinion in the labour movement. The earliest measures, school meals and compulsory school medical inspection, originated in bills introduced by Labour backbenchers[83] and had been the subject of campaigns by the SDF, trades councils and the Women's Co-operative Guild long before the revelations of working-class physical debility during the Boer War.[84] The Old Age Pensions Act of 1908 also followed long campaigns in the labour movement and elsewhere, though it can only be interpreted as at most a partial satisfaction of their aims. 'Well begun—half done!' as Rogers put it.[85] The response among pensioners themselves was divided. Though some new pensioners, such as those quoted in Flora Thompson's *Lark Rise*, thanked 'that Lord George' for the new pension,[86] other pensioners or workers grumbled that it was 'too little, too late'; *The Times* reported that, when mentioned at public meetings, the pension was greeted by 'ironical cheers'.[87] It was entirely consistent to hold both views at once. Of course it was better to have 5s. at 70 than a choice between destitution and the work-house. Five hundred thousand very poor, very old people came forward for the pension in 1909 who, to qualify under the stringent means test, must previously have been in penury. But it was reasonable to feel that they deserved more, earlier in life. The Liverpool Trades Council described the pension as 'an insult and a mockery to the veterans of industry'.[88]

These early Liberal reforms can be attributed to successful Labour pressure to the extent that it is highly unlikely that they would have been implemented at all but for the existence of an increasingly well-organised labour movement, which posed a real threat to the political *status quo*; but the reforms cannot simply be interpreted as a direct result of Labour pressure. They were far from being complete victories for Labour; they were granted very much on Liberal terms. They contained controls and limitations which were closer to the demands of politicians like Chamberlain and employers in the Chamber of Commerce[89] than those of the labour movement.[90]

Many working people were critical of the early Liberal measures and disappointed with Labour's performance in parliament, but the trades councils, Women's Co-operative Guilds and other local organisations strove whenever possible for representation in the administration, and to ensure that as far as possible they were

administered in the working-class interest—a participation which
the Liberal government encouraged, to some extent as a means
of containing working-class criticism.

There were more important splits over the later national
insurance legislation. The Parliamentary Labour Party was
divided about the principle of national insurance. The majority
followed Ramsay MacDonald, who supported it on the grounds
that non-contributory welfare would split the working class, by
making only lower-paid workers subject to state charity when in
need, and therefore less likely to join with the rest of the working
class to fight to improve conditions.[91] Others, including Philip
Snowden, argued that national insurance was undesirable in
principle because it placed part of the burden of the cost on the
workers themselves through their contributions and through
increased prices, as employers passed on their contributions,[92]
and because it was wrong to demand regular contributions from
low-paid and irregularly employed workers. The latter group
included many women. The Women's Trade Union League
campaigned against contributory pensions before 1908 and
against national insurance before 1911,[93] in company with the
Women's Co-operative Guild and the Women's Labour League.
The latter was founded in 1906 and campaigned for a variety of
advanced reforms, especially on behalf of women, and also, with
some success, encouraged participation by working women on
elected and appointed public bodies.[94]

MacDonald appears to have undergone an entirely genuine
crisis of conscience over support for reforms which he recognised
might be capitalist stratagems, but he feared to alienate Liberal
trade unionists if he opposed them, not to mention the mass
working-class vote, when Labour had not yet the power to put
anything in its place. To do this, he argued, was precisely to play
into Liberal hands, enabling the Liberals to present themselves
as the benefactors of the working class whilst Labour would
appear to be the betrayers. Labour was in a familiar dilemma; it
too could apparently neither conscientiously support nor
successfully oppose Liberal welfare.[95] Few alternative political
strategies were available, though by 1911 the trade union
movement was surging into a new phase of growth, militancy and
optimism.

Increasingly sophisticated arguments in their favour made the
Liberal reforms still harder for Labour to resist; that welfare

benefits, by increasing consumption, would increase employment; that pensions would do the same by withdrawing older
workers from the labour force.[96] Hence the stance most characteristic of organised labour after 1906 was one of support for the
Liberal reforms whilst stressing their inadequacy, and pressing
both for improvement and for maximum working-class participation in their administration to achieve further gains. Unwillingness to compromise with the Liberal reforms by 1912 characterised only the most radical socialists and the most radical
individualist Liberals. For these, the National Insurance and
Labour Exchanges Acts were further steps in the growth of the
centralising state and the enslavement of the worker at his or her
own expense. This view was most clearly expressed in the *Daily
Herald*, which returned to the theme repeatedly in the first two
years of its existence under George Lansbury's editorship, from
April 1912. The *Herald* interpreted labour exchanges not as an
attempt to minimise unemployment by providing information
about vacancies and making them available to the unemployed,
but as a first move in the compulsory registration of labour, to
bring about the future direction of labour in the interests of the
employing classes, and as a possible source of blackleg labour for
strikebound employers.[97] It also criticised the inquisitorial
administration of the earlier measures, such as the stigmatisa-
tion of schoolchildren qualifying for free meals, even, as Lansbury commented, by working-class elected representatives.[98]

The introduction of unemployment insurance seemed to
increase the plausibility of this interpretation. In the *Herald's*
eyes this was the beginning of the process of registering and
controlling all workers, of keeping complete work records
ultimately for use against them. They interpreted the combined
labour exchange and unemployment insurance legislation as a
conscious plot hatched between Lloyd George and the employers,
the preparation for a new offensive against the labour movement.
They described the employers as bitterly disappointed by the
reversal of the Taff Vale judgement in the Trade Disputes Act,
1906, recognising the impossibility of trying another similar
assault on labour through the law courts and approaching Lloyd
George instead with this new, more subtle plot for the enslavement of labour. This would give them unprecedented control over
the labour force and knowledge of its movements which would
enable them to prepare for a confrontation, to smash labour at
its weakest.[99]

Strictly and literally, there was little truth in this interpretation—the unemployment legislation was indeed the work of
Churchill, not of Lloyd George. There is no evidence of a con-
certed plot of these dimensions; but it was not total fantasy.
Blacklegs recruited through labour exchanges were employed in
a railway strike in 1913, though there was an immediate outcry,
and there is no evidence that it was done again (but the subject
has not been adequately researched).[100] It is probably fair to
assume that many employers would willingly have acquiesced in
this use of the new system.

The *Herald's* view was repeated in the pages of *Justice* and
Clarion. It was echoed in the writings of the liberal Hilaire Belloc,
whose *The Servile State*, published in 1912, was an attack upon
the limitations imposed upon individual freedom by the growth
of centralised bureaucracy. Belloc expounded his views also in
the *Daily Herald* and on public platforms alongside Lansbury—
who found such activities compatible with his role of radical poor
law guardian in Poplar. Together, they advocated a boycott of
national insurance and refusal to register at labour exchanges,
with very little success.[101] There were one or two strikes against
compulsory deductions and contributions, a few workers and
employers were fined for refusal to comply with the Act, but little
else that even the *Herald* could detect. Suspicion of the unemployment legislation was initially widespread, among trades
councils for example,[102] but it was defused after 1911 by the
appointment of trade unionists to the directorships of some
labour exchanges, to local insurance committees and to the
labour department of the Board of Trade.[103] Complicated
provision was made to include unskilled, lower-paid workers in
the unemployment insurance scheme. Trade unions could, if
they wished, administer state benefits to their members.[104]

The Board of Trade worked hard to win working-class support,
sending speakers to trades councils and other organisations to
convince them of the government's benign intentions. They did
not have a difficult task to win over the mass of moderate
members. Even those who had opposed the contributory
insurance principle preferred, once it was in operation, to try to
work with it and to influence administration as far as possible in
the working-class interest.[105] The insurance legislation, as Lloyd
George intended, and Lenin noted, exacerbated the split in the
labour movement between radical critics of state welfare, and its
willing and unwilling supporters. The latter were in the majority.

Although 'servile state' notions may have been theoretically appealing to many working people, and they clearly belonged to the traditions of ideas apparent in the SDF and among many working-class liberals, they were not sufficiently strong rooted to arouse widespread opposition to the Liberal measures before 1914.

Conclusion

So what does this partial, selective and hurried survey tell us about working-class attitudes to welfare before 1914? That there was, as Pelling suggested, widespread suspicion of the policies and actions of Liberal and other politicians. The grounds for this suspicion were that they were too limited, too 'intrusive', and a threat to working-class independence both collective and individual. But these views were not universal and probably diminished over time. Many poorer people, throughout, were grateful for any amelioration of hard lives. It is reasonable to conclude that very many people would have preferred, as an ideal, regular work, wages sufficient for a decent life, however defined, allowing them sufficient surplus to save for hard times and perhaps even to choose and pay for their children's education, their own house, or health care, leaving the state the minimal role of providing services which the individual could not, and for the minority who were unable for physical or other reasons to achieve this desirable independence. Only a highly politicised minority of liberals and socialists thought with any precision about the desirable extent and nature of state action. Few however could have thought either the individualist or collectivist versions of this desirable state foreseeably attainable before 1914. Hence the divided views as to the alternative. In Britain, as elsewhere, working-class support for state welfare strengthened with Labour's chances of attaining local or central power. Hence their greater support for state action from the 1920s on, as Labour became a governing party at local and central level.

Notes

David Gladstone

1   Finlayson, G. *Citizen, State and Social Welfare in Britain 1830-1990*, Oxford: Clarendon Press,1994, p 3.

2   Daunton, M., *Charity, Self Interest and Welfare in the English Past*, London: UCL Press,1996, p. 1.

3   Finlayson, G., 'A moving frontier: voluntarism and the state in British social welfare', *Twentieth Century British History*, Vol.1, No. 2, 1990.

4   This distinction was first made by Le Grand, J. and Robinson, R. in *Privatisation and the Welfare State*, London: George Allen and Unwin, 1984, pp. 3-5.

5   Baldwin, P., *The Politics of Social Solidarity*, Cambridge: Cambridge University Press,1990, p. 37.

6   The terminology is that of Wilensky, H.L. and Lebeaux, C.N. in *Industrial Society and Social Welfare*, Glencoe, Illinois: The Free Press, 1965, pp. 138-47.

7   Johnson, P., 'The welfare state' in Floud, R. and McCloskey, D. (eds.), *The Economic History of Britain since 1700*, second edn., Cambridge: Cambridge University, Vol. 3, 1994, p. 287.

8   Glennerster, H., 'Social policy since the Second World War' in Hills, J. (ed.), *The State of Welfare*, Oxford: Clarendon Press, 1990, p. 11.

9   Webster, C., *The Health Services Since the War*, London: HMSO, 1988, Vol. I, p. 2.

10 Thane, P., 'Government and society in England and Wales,1750-1914', in Thompson, F.M.L. (ed.), *The Cambridge Social History of Britain 1750-1950*, Cambridge: Cambridge University Press, 1990, Vol. 3, p. 19.

11 Thane, P., *Foundations of the Welfare State*, second edn., London: Longman, 1996, p. 28.

12 Johnson, P., *Saving and Spending: The Working Class Economy in Britain 1870-1939*, Oxford: Clarendon Press,1985, p. 55.

13 Fraser, D., *The Evolution of the British Welfare State*, second edn., London: Macmillan, 1984, pp.161-64; Thane, *Foundations of the Welfare State, op. cit.*, pp. 78-88.

14 Thane, *Foundations of the Welfare State, op. cit.*, p. 88.

15 Fraser, D., *The Evolution of the British Welfare State, op. cit.*, pp.163-64.

16 Green, D.G., *Community without Politics: A Market Approach to Welfare Reform*, London: IEA Health and Welfare Unit,1996, pp.131-32.

17 Green, D.G., *Reinventing Civil Society*, London: IEA Health and Welfare Unit, 1993, Ch. 9.

18 Daunton, *Charity, Self Interest and Welfare in the English Past, op. cit.*, p. 13.

19 Green, *Reinventing Civil Society, op. cit.*, p. 120.

20 Harris, J., *Private Lives, Public Spirit: A Social History of Britain 1870-1914*, Oxford: Oxford University Press, 1993, p. 240; See also Lewis, J., *The Voluntary Sector, the State and Social Work in Britain*, Aldershot: Edward Elgar, 1995, Part I, *passim*; and Gladstone, D., 'Locating the Bosanquets: state, society and welfare in late Victorian and Edwardian Britain' in Gladstone, D. (ed.), *Helen and Bernard Bosanquet, Works on Economics and Social Welfare*, London: Routledge, 1996. Vol. I, pp. vii-lxvi.

21 Field, F., *Reforming Welfare*, London: Social Market Foundation, 1997, p. 48.

Jane Lewis

1 Paci, M., 'Long waves in the development of welfare systems', in Maier, C.S. (ed.), *Changing Boundaries of the Political: Essays on the Evolving Balance between State and Society, Public and Private in Europe*, Cambridge: Cambridge University Press, 1987.

2 Titmuss, R.M., *Essays on the Welfare State*, London: Allen and Unwin, 1963.

3 Oakley, A., 'Social welfare and the position of women', Richard Titmuss Memorial Lecture, Hebrew University of Jerusalem, 1986.

4 Le Grand, J. and Bartlett, W., *Quasi-Markets and Social Policy*, London: Macmillan, 1983.

5 Esping Andersen, G., *The Three Worlds of Welfare Capitalism*, Cambridge: Polity Press, 1990.

6 Kuhnle, S. and Selle, P., 'Government and voluntary organisations: a relational perspective', in Kuhnle, S. and Selle, P. (eds.), *Government and Voluntary Organisations*, Aldershot: Avebury, 1992.

7 Hansmann, H., 'Economic theories of non profit organisations', in Powell, W.W. (ed.), *The Non Profit Sector: A Research Handbook*, New Haven: Yale University Press, 1987.

8   Weisbrod, B.A., *The Nonprofit Economy*, Cambridge, Mass: Harvard University Press, 1988.

9   Kuhnle and Selle, *op. cit.*

10   Salamon, L.M., 'Partners in public service: the scope and theory of government: non-profit relations', in Powell, W.W. (ed.), *The Non Profit Sector: A Research Handbook*, New Haven: Yale University Press, 1987; Salamon, L.M., 'The non-profit sector and government in the US', in Anheier, H.K. and Seibel, W. (eds.), *The Third Sector: Comparative Studies of Non-profit Organizations*, New York: Aldine de Gruyter, 1990.

11   Gronjberg, K., 'Patterns of institutional relations in the welfare state: public mandates and the nonprofit sector', *Journal of Voluntary Action Research*, Vol. 16, 1987.

12   Ware, A., 'Meeting needs through voluntary action: does market society corrode altruism?', in Ware, A. and Goodin, R.E. (eds.), *Needs and Welfare*, London: Sage, 1990.

13   This section draws on Lewis, J., *The Voluntary Sector, the State and Social Work in Britain*, Aldershot: Edward Elgar, 1995.

14   Harris, J., *Private Lives, Public Spirit: A Social History of Britain, 1870-1914*, Oxford: Oxford University Press, 1993.

15   Yeo, S., *Religion and Voluntary Organisations in Crisis*, London: Croom Helm, 1976.

16   Harris, J., 'Society and the state in twentieth century Britain', in Thompson, F.M.L. (ed.), *The Cambridge Social History of Britain 1750-1950*, Vol. 3, Social Agencies and Institutions, Cambridge: Cambridge University Press, 1990, p. 67.

17   Thane, P., 'Government and society in England and Wales, 1750-1914', in Thompson, *The Cambridge Social History of Britain, 1750-1950*, *op. cit.*, p. 1.

18   Willetts, D., *Modern Conservatism*, Harmondsworth: Penguin, 1992.

19   Finlayson, G., 'A moving frontier: voluntarism and the state in British social welfare', *Twentieth Century British History*, Vol. 1, No. 2, 1990.

20   Webb, B. and Webb, S., *The Prevention of Destitution*, London: by the authors, 1912.

21   Macadam, E., *The New Philanthropy: A Study of the Relations Between the Statutory and Voluntary Social Services*, London: George Allen and Unwin, 1934.

22   Beveridge, Lord, *Voluntary Action: A Report on Methods of Social Advance*, London: George Allen & Unwin, 1948.

David G. Green

1   Taking out unregistered friendly societies, there were 6.6 million registered members of friendly societies and 2.5 million registered trade union members.

2   Hayek, F.A., *The Constitution of Liberty*, London: Routledge, 1960.

3   For a fuller account see Green, D.G., *Reinventing Civil Society*, London: IEA, 1993.

4   Gosden, P.H.J.H., *The Friendly Societies in England 1815-1875*, Manchester: Manchester University Press, 1961, pp. 4-5.

5   Gosden, *Self-Help*, London: Batsford, 1973, p. 91; Beveridge, Lord, *Voluntary Action: A Report on Methods of Social Advance*, London: George Allen & Unwin, 1948, p. 328.

6   Ancient Order of Foresters, Lecture 3, 1879, pp. 50-51.

7   Ancient Order of Foresters, Lecture 1, 1879, pp. 41-42.

Noel Whiteside

1   Whiteside, N., 'Unemployment and health: an historical perspective', *Journal of Social Policy*, Vol. 12, pp. 177-94. Also Whiteside, N., *Bad Times: Unemployment in British Social and Political History*, Faber & Faber, 1991, ch.4.

2   See, e.g., Honigsbaum, F., *The Division in British Medicine*, London: Kogan Page, 1979; Fox, D.M., *Health Policies, Health Politics*, New Jersey: Princeton University Press, 1986; Eder, N.R., *National Health Insurance and the Medical Profession in Britain, 1913-39*, New York: Garland Publishing, 1982; Digby, A. and Bosanquet, N., 'Doctors and patients in an era of national health insurance and private practice', *Economic History Review*, Vol. 41 No. 1, 1988.

3   *Social Insurance and Allied Services*, Cmd. 6404 and Cmd. 6405., 1942. Hereafter Beveridge Report.

4   E.g., Honigsbaum, *The Division in British Medicine, op. cit.*; Gilbert, B.B., *British Social Policy, 1914-39*, London: Batsford, 1966.

5   Political and Economic Planning (PEP), *Report on the British Health Services*, London: P.E.P., 1937, pp. 198-99.

6   Ministry of Health, *National Health Insurance and Contributory Pensions Insurance*, London: HMSO, 1939, pp. 32-34.

7   Beveridge Report, Tables I and II, Cmd. 6404, 1942, p. 25.

8 Government Actuary, 'Memo on Beveridge's Heads of Scheme (1941)': ACT 1/685, Public Record Office.

9 A detailed account of NHI finances is in Whiteside, N., 'Private Agencies and Public Purposes', *Journal of Social Policy*, Vol. 12, No. 2, 1983, pp. 165-94; also Whiteside, N., 'Regulating Markets' *Public Administration*, Vol. 75, No. 3, 1997, pp. 467-85.

10 Kinnear to Minister: memo 26 February 1942: PIN 4/11, Public Record Office.

11 Ministry of Health, *National Health Insurance and Contributory Pensions Insurance*, London: HMSO, 1939, pp. 14-15.

12 Government Actuary, *Widows', Orphans and Old-Age Pensions Bill: Report*, Cmd. 2406, 1925, pp. 17-18: ACT 1/247, Public Record Office.

13 Papers on files ACT 1/483: PIN 3/117, Public Record Office.

14 AGM: NATUAS, 1930, p. 9: MSS 292 155/1: Modern Records Centre Medical Research Council, Warwick.

15 Papers on file PIN 4/11and MH 62/34, Public Record Office.

16 E.g., The Kent Miners Benefit Society lapsed into deficit in the early 1920s; repeated requests by official auditors to correct matters were ignored, approval was withdrawn in 1927, the members being transferred to the Tunbridge Wells Friendly and Equitable.

17 Evidence, Wright, 18 March 1914, *Evidence to the Departmental Committee on Sickness Benefit Claims*, PP. XXXI, Cd. 7689, pp. 77, 78.

18 Whiteside, 'Private Agencies and Public Purposes', *op. cit.*

19 Deacon, A., *In Search of the Scrounger*, London: London School of Economics, 1977.

20 Papers in ACT 1/247 and PIN 1/1-2, Public Record Office.

21 Whiteside, 'Regulating Markets' *op. cit.*

22 Political and Economic Planning, *Report on the British Health Services*, *op. cit.*, p. 201.

23 Deputation TUC to Ministry of Health, January 1937: MSS 292/ 152/3, Medical Research Council.

24 Peters, 22 October 1913, *Evidence to the Departmental Committee on Sickness Benefit Claims*, PP. XXX, *op. cit.*, p. 53.

25 Evidence of National Conference Industrial Insurance Approved Societies to Beveridge Committee, 25 March 1942: CAB 87/77 Public Record Office.

26   Chairman's Report to AGM, 12 May 1913, p. 71: PIN 24/153 Public Record Office.

27   Tunbridge Wells Equitable Approved Society Minutes, 23 July 1930: PIN 24/167 Public Record Office.

28   *The Equitable*, No. 126: PIN 24/169, Public Record Office.

29   The Tunbridge Wells Equitable Approved Society's financially astute secretary made substantial funds from investments. PIN 24/153, Public Record Office.

30   Most had to amend their rules to comply with the legislation, requiring ratification at their annual conferences; this provoked delay. Levine (actuary) to Ramsay Macdonald, October 1911: 'Report on effects of the National Insurance Bill on Trade Unions', T 1/11335/19413/1911, Public Record Office.

31   TUC delegate conference on social insurance, October 1928; Scottish TUC September, 1929: MSS 292 154/4: Medical Research Council.

32   Beveridge draft, p. 56 (n.d. 1942); BP VIII/36/17, British Library of Political and Economic Science.

33   Beveridge, memorandum to War Cabinet, 20 August 1942, pp. 2-3; BP VIII/36/21, British Library of Political and Economic Science.

34   Prudential memorandum to Beveridge Committee, May 1942; BP VIII/36/31, p. 2, British Library of Political and Economic Science.

35   Harris, J., *William Beveridge*, Oxford: Clarendon Press, 1977, ch. 16.

36   Report of the Departmental Committee on Sickness Benefit Claims, Cd. 7687, PP XXX, 1914-16, p. 26.

37   Barber (Bradford and District Trades Council), 4 March 1914, Evidence to Departmental Committee on Sickness Benefit Claims, *op. cit.*, PP XXX, 1914-16, pp. 458-59.

38   Evidence, *op. cit.*, 18 March 1914, PP XXXI, p. 71, Q. 31794.

39   E.g., TUC evidence, 14 January 1942, p. 35, CAB 87/77, Public Record Office.

40   Evidence to Beveridge by the National Confederation of Industrial Insurance Approved Societies, 25 March 1942, p. 30, CAB 87/77, Public Record Office.

41   Tunbridge Wells Equitable Approved Society Minutes, 23 July 1912, PIN 24/153, Public Record Office.

42   Tunbridge Wells Equitable Approved Society AGM Report, May 1914, loc. cit.

43 Minutes, 23 October 1915, p. 192, *loc. cit.*

44 Epps to Beveridge, 1 July 1942, BP VIII/30/3, British Library of Political and Economic Science.

45 Public and Economic Planning, *Report on the British Health Services, op. cit.,* p. 204.

46 Royal Commission on National Health Insurance, Cmd. 2596, 1926, pp. 65-66; also Appendix XXVI, pp. 291-92.

47 Fox, *Health Policies, Health Politics, op. cit.*, ch. 2.

48 Macnalty, memorandum, March 1937, pp. 5-14: MH 79/409, Public Record Office; Public and Economic Planning, *Report on the British Health Services, op. cit.*, pp. 181-84.

49 Committee on Scottish Health Services, *Report*, Cmd. 5204, PP XI, 1934-5, p. 236 and pp. 156-57.

50 *Op. cit.*

51 London County Council, *LCC Hospitals, A Retrospect*, London: Staples Press, 1949; Ministry of Health, *London Health Services*, London: HMSO, 1936.

52 Beveridge, W.H., *Insurance for All and Everything*, pamphlet, London, 1924.

53 Papers on file BP VIII/44/65, British Library of Political and Economic Science.

54 'Heads of Scheme for Social Security', December 1941, BP VIII/27/8, British Library of Political and Economic Science.

55 Government Actuary's papers, cover 7, p. 7; ACT 1/688, Public Record Office.

56 Beveridge minutes: CAB 87/77, Public Record Office.

57 Beveridge notes on evidence; BP VIII/ 27/113, British Library of Political and Economic Science.

58 Papers on file BP VIII/53, British Library of Political and Economic Science.

59 Notes: BP VIII/53/70, British Library of Political and Economic Science.

60 Lincoln, J., *The Way Ahead*, pamphlet, 1946.

61 Davies (Labour MP for East Ham North) to House of Commons Committee A on the National Insurance Bill, 21 March 1946, p.331: BP VIII/53/79, British Library of Political and Economic Science. This debate over approved society participation continued for three days.

62   See defence of Bill before HC Standing Committee A, March 1946, by Griffiths (Minister of National Insurance) and Lindgreen (Parliamentary Secretary).

63   Labour Party memo, June 1945, copy on file BP VIII/53/42, British Library of Political and Economic Science.

64   Local Government Manpower Committee, 1949: papers in HLG 52/1733; report (unpublished) in T 214/244—both Public Record Office. Also Royal Commission on the Civil Service, *Report*, PP XI, 1955-6, Cmd 9613.

Jose Harris

1   Prest, A.R. and Adams, A.A., *Consumers' Expenditure in the United Kingdom 1900-1919*, Cambridge: Cambridge University Press, 1954 p. 162; Mitchell, B.R. and Deane, P., *Abstract of British Historical Statistics*, Cambridge: Cambridge University Press, 1962, p. 418.

2   On the differing structures of modern welfare states, see Flora, P. and Heidenheimer, A.J. (eds.), *The Development of Welfare States in Europe and America*, New Brunswick, 1981; Flora, P. (ed.), *Growth to Limits: The Western European Welfare States Since World War Two*, New York and Berlin, 1987, i, ii, iv *passim*.

3   See in particular the introduction to Dicey, A.V., *Lectures on the Relation between Law and Public Opinion in England during the Nineteenth Century*, second edn., London: Macmillan, 1914, pp. xxiii-xciv.

4   Brebner, J., 'Laissez-faire and state intervention in nineteenth century Britain', *Journal of Economic History*, Supplement No. 8, 1948, pp. 59-73; Hart, J., 'Nineteenth-century social reform: a Tory interpretation of history', *Past and Present*, No. 31, July 1965, pp. 39-61.

5   Goldman, L., 'A peculiarity of the English? The Social Science Association and the absence of sociology in nineteenth-century Britain', *Past and Present*, No. 114, February 1987, pp. 133-71.

6   Freeden, M., 'Eugenics and progressive thought: a study in ideological affinity', *History Journal*, Vol. xxii, 1979, pp. 645-71.

7   MacBriar, A.M., *An Edwardian Mixed Doubles: The Bosanquets versus the Webbs: A Study in British Social Policy, 1890-1929*, Oxford: Clarendon Press, 1987.

8   Mackenzie, D.M., *Statistics in Britain, 1865-1930: The Social Construction of Scientific Knowledge*, Edinburgh: Edinburgh University Press, 1981; Szretzer, S.R.S., 'The first scientific social structure of modern Britain', in Bonfield, L., Smith, R.M. and Wrightson, K., (eds.), *The World We Have Gained: Histories of*

Population and Social Structure, Oxford: Oxford University Press, 1986, pp. 337-54.

9   Topalov, C., 'Invention du chômage et politiques sociales au début du siècle', *Temps Modernes*, Nos. 496-97, November-December 1987, pp. 54-92.

10 Goldman, L., 'The Social Science Association, 1857-1886: a context for mid-Victorian liberalism', *English Historical Review*, ci., 1986, pp. 99-154. Throughout this article I have used the term 'positivism' (meaning an approach to social explanation derived from the natural sciences) as distinct from 'Positivism' (meaning an adherent of the Positivist movement founded by August Comte).

11 *Ibid.*, pp. 128-30. For a rather different interpretation, emphasising the accidental nature of the Social Science Association's collapse, and the subsequent continuity of its intellectual and policy concerns, see Rodgers, B., 'The Social Science Association', *Manchester School*, Vol. xx, 1952, pp. 283-310.

12 An invaluable source of information on these bodies is the quarterly journal, *Progress: Civic, Social and Industrial: The Organ of the British Institute of Social Service*, founded in 1906. Its patrons included several earls and bishops, but the backbone of both journal and institute was a large group of progressive Nonconformist liberals, headed by J.B. Paton, George Cadbury, Percy Alden, G.P. Gooch, J.A. Hobson and B.S. Rowntree. The cover of *Progress*, a gothic woodcut of St George, is a useful reminder that the emblems of patriotism and civic virtue in this period were not the monopoly of imperialists and conservatives.

13 *Progress* included contributions from all these strands of reformist thought; and the practical activities of the different strands reveal the community of interests between them. Paton, for example, was the main promoter of British 'Elberfeld' schemes (a system of civic neighbourhood visiting usually associated with the COS). For a revealing account of local co-operation between the COS and the socialist groups, see C.H. Grinling, *Fifty Years of Pioneer Work in Woolwich*, Woolwich: Pioneer Press, 1922.

14 *Proceedings of the National Conference on the Prevention of Destitution*, London, 1912, 11-14 June 1912.

15 Macadam, E., *The Equipment of the Social Worker*, London: Allen and Unwin, 1925, pp. 6-54.

16 Mairet, P., *Pioneer of Sociology: The Life and Letters of Patrick Geddes*, London: Lund Humphries, 1957; Branford, Mrs V., 'Civic revival: an account of the progress of civic societies', *Sociological Review*, Vol. xiv, 1923, p. 41.

17   This judgement takes issue with the argument of Philip Abrams, *The Origins of British Sociology, 1834-1914*, Chicago and London: University of Chicago Press, 1968, pp. 107-13.

18   See Cahill, M. and Jowitt, T., 'The new philanthropy; the emergence of the Bradford City Guild of Help', *Journal of Social Policy*, Vol. ix, 1980, pp. 359-82.

19   Macadam, *The Equipment of the Social Worker, op. cit.*, pp. 15-53.

20   I have used the term 'idealist' in a very broad sense, to refer not just to philosophers who self-consciously adhered to the Idealist school, but to anyone who thought that knowledge rested on certain *a priori* categories, who viewed society and/or the state as having a real corporate identity, and who saw the prime concerns of social science as being the interpretation of 'meaning' and 'purpose' rather than the discovery of causal laws.

21   For example, Rowntree, B.S., *Land and Labour: Lessons from Belgium*, London: Macmillan, 1911, p. 535.

22   Collini, S., 'Sociology and Idealism in Britain, 1880-1920', *European Journal of Sociology*, Vol. xix, 1978, pp. 3-30, suggests that the antipathy between Idealism and evolutionary sociology was one of the factors that thwarted the growth of a strong school of sociological theory in Britain. But though this antipathy may have characterised the generation of Herbert Spencer, it was much less evident in the generation of Hobhouse, Branford and Geddes, all of whom were strongly influenced by Idealist concerns. Moreover Bernard Bosanquet, doyen of Edwardian Idealists, took a leading role in introducing the ideas of Durkheim into English social thought. Collini himself notes the affinities between the two schools in his 'Hobhouse, Bosanquet and the State: Philosophical Idealism and Political Argument in England, 1880-1981', *Past and Present*, No. 72, August 1976, pp. 86-111.

23   Urwick, E.J., *A Philosophy of Social Progress*, London: Methuen, 1912,; Urwick, E.J., *The Social Good*, London: Methuen, 1927. Urwick was unusual among British Idealists in that, although he invoked Idealist metaphysics and modes of argument, he rejected the possibility of the real corporate personality of the state.

24   Urwick himself subsequently became professor of economics and head of the school of social work at the University of Toronto. One of his best-known pupils was C.B. Macpherson, author of *The Political Theory of Possessive Individualism: Hobbes to Locke*, Oxford: Oxford University Press, 1962, whose early writings acknowledged a major debt to Urwick's thought.

25   St. John Heath, J., 'Training courses for social work', *Progress*, No. 26, April 1912, pp. 88-96.

26 Harris, J., 'The Webbs, the COS and the Ratan Tata Foundation', in Bulmer, M., Lewis, J. and Piachaud, D. (eds.), *The Goals of Social Policy*, London: Unwin Hyam, 1989. pp. 27-63.

27 See, for example, the debate on the Poor Law Commission between Bosanquet, Tom Jones, James Seth and others in *International Journal of Ethics*, Vols. xx-xxii, 1909-12, *passim*.

28 This point is much more fully explored in Sandra den Otter, 'The search for a "social philosophy": the Idealists of late Victorian and Edwardian Britain', University of Oxford, D. Phil. thesis, 1990.

29 Willis, K., 'The introduction and critical reception of Hegelian thought in Britain, 1830-1900', *Victorian Studies*, Vol. xxxii, 1988, pp. 85-111.

30 The so-called 'Hegelians' of the Charity Organisation Society, for example, were apparently unaware of Hegel's view that charity and social welfare were fully 'rational' only insofar as they were depersonalized and automatic. 'Public social conditions are ... to be regarded as all the more perfect the less [in comparison with what is arranged publicly] is left for an individual to do by himself as his private inclination directs'. [Hegel, G.F., *The Philosophy of Right*, trans. Knox, T.M., Oxford: Oxford University Press, 1967 edn., p.149.]

31 See Barker, E., *Political Thought in England, 1848-1914*, Oxford: Oxford University Press, 1915, pp. 217-21; Cole, G.D.H., introduction to the Everyman edn. of Rousseau, J.J., *The Social Contract* and *The Discourses*, London: Dutton, 1913, reprinted 1973, pp. xi-xliv.

32 Tuner, F.M., *The Greek Heritage in Victorian Britain*, New Haven: Yale University Press, 1981, ch. 8.

33 See, for example, Jones, Sir Henry, *The Working Faith of the Social Reformers and Other Essays*, London: Macmillan, 1910, pp. 273-77.

34 Crossman, R.H., *Plato Today*, London: 1937; Popper, K., *The Open Society and Its Enemies*, Vol. I, *The Spell of Plato*, Princeton: Princeton University Press, 1963, first published 1945, pp. 194-201.

35 McDougall, W., *An Introduction to Social Psychology*, 20th edn., London: Methuen, 1924; McDougall, W., *Ethics and Some Modern World Problems*, New York: Putnam, 1924; McDougall, W., *The Group Mind*, Cambridge: Cambridge University Press, 1927. For an analysis of McDougall's thought, see Soffer, R., *Ethics and Society in England: The Revolution in the Social Sciences, 1870-1914*, Berkeley: University of California Press, 1978, pp. 217-51.

36 Bosanquet, B., *A Companion to Plato's Republic*, London: 1895, p. 21.

37   See, for example, Bosanquet, *Companion to Plato's Republic, op. cit.*; Urwick, E.J., *The Message of Plato: A Re-Interpretation of the Republic*, London: Methuen, 1920; Mackenzie, J.S., 'Spiritual values', *International Journal of Ethics*, xxxiii, 1922-23, pp. 248-57; Muirhead, J.H., *The Platonic Tradition in Anglo-Saxon Philosophy*, London: Allen and Unwin, 1931.

38   Bosanquet, B., 'The meaning of social work', *International Journal of Ethics*, Vol. xi, 1900-01, p. 294.

39   Urwick, *Message of Plato, op. cit.*

40   Jones, T., 'Pauperism: facts and theories', *International Journal of Ethics*, Vol. xx, 1909-10, p. 198.

41   *Progress*, No. 22, January 1911, p. 97; No. 24, July 1911, p. 168; No. 73, July-September 1926, pp. 1-2; No. 81, July-September 1928, pp. 4-8.

42   Fairbrother, W.H., rev. of English translation of Gomperz, T., *Greek Thinkers*, in *International Journal of Ethics*, Vol. xii, 1901-02, p. 198. The journal, published initially in Philadelphia, later in Chicago, was edited by a joint committee of British and American philosophers. Between the 1890s and 1930s it published a continuous stream of articles on the application of classical and modern Idealist philosophy to current political, ethical and 'social welfare' issues.

43   White, E.M., 'The purpose of civics and how it is served in recent English textbooks', *Sociological Review*, Vol. xv, 1923, p. 209.

44   Dawson, C., 'Progress and decay in ancient and modern civilization', *Sociological Review*, Vol. xvi, 1924, pp. 1-10.

45   'Quality or Quantity', reports of lectures to an Oxford Summer School by Sir Wyndham Deedes and Sir Donald McAlister, *Social Service Review*, Vol. xi, 1930, pp. 159-60. See also Myres, J.L., 'The science of man in the service of the state', *Social Services Review*, Vol. xi, 1930, pp. 230-35, 249-53, Vol. xii, 1931, pp. 1-6.

46   Owen, A.D.K., 'The social survey of a city', *Social Service Review*, Vol. xi, 1930, pp. 186-91; see also Farquharson, A., 'Community surveys for new housing estates', *Social Services Review*, Vol. xi, 1930, pp. 115-18.

47   Presland, J., 'Freedom and Planning', *Social Services Review*, Vol. xiv, 1933, pp. 19-23.

48   *Sociological Review*, Vol. xxiii, 1931, pp. 1-14.

49   Vincent, A., and Plant, R., *Philosophy, Politics and Citizenship: The Life and Thought of the British Idealists*, Oxford: Basil Blackwell, 1984, ch. 6.

50   Bosanquet, H., *The Strength of the People*, second edn., London:
        Macmillan, 1903, p. 107.

51   Bosanquet, B., 'Charity Organisation and the Majority Report',
        International Journal of Ethics, Vol. xx, 1901-10, p. 396. In fact
        Bosanquet's perception was inaccurate on this point; it was
        precisely in the concept of a citizen mind that many Fabians,
        particularly the Webbs, came surprisingly close to the Idealist
        position.

52   Bosanquet, B., *The Philosophical Theory of the State*, London:
        Macmillan, 1899, pp. 296-334.

53   Beatrice's diary recorded 'our total inability to sympathize with or
        even understand' Hegelian metaphysics [*The Diary of Beatrice
        Webb, iv, 1924-1943*, Norman and Jeanne Mckenzie (eds.),
        London: Virago, 1985, p. 72]; but the diaries are nevertheless
        studded with conceptions like 'state-conscious idealism' and
        'genuinely state-conscious collective mind'. The Idealist bent in
        Sidney's thought is perhaps most clearly apparent in his article on
        'Social movements', in Ward, A.W., Protheroe, G.W. and Leathes,
        S. (eds.), *Cambridge Modern History*, 13 Vols., Cambridge:
        Cambridge University Press, 1902-11, Vol. xii, pp. 730-65.

54   Seth, J., 'The problem of destitution: a plea for the Minority
        Report', *International Journal of Ethics*, Vol. xxii, 1911-12, pp. 39-
        50. Seth was the brother of a more famous late Victorian Idealist
        philosopher, Andrew Pringle-Pattison.

55   Jones, T., 'Pauperism: facts and theories', *op. cit.*

56   Attlee, C., *The Modern Social Worker*, London, 1919; Greenwood,
        A., 'A plea for voluntary service', *Social Services Review*, Vol. xi,
        1930, p. 161; Harris, 'Webbs, the COS and the Ratan Tata
        Foundation', *op. cit.*; Thane, P., 'Labour and local politics:
        radicalism, democracy and social reform, 1880-1914', in Biagini,
        E. and Reid, A. (eds.), *Currents of Radicalism: Popular Radicalism,
        Organized Labour and Party Politics in Britain, 1850-1914*,
        Cambridge: Cambridge University Press, 1991, pp. 244-70;
        Henderson, A., 'The character and policy of the British Labour
        Party', *International Journal of Ethics*, Vol. xxxii, 1921-2, p. 119.

57   Owen, 'Social survey of a city', *op. cit.*, pp. 186-91.

58   Astbury, B.E. 'A restatement of casework', an address to the
        Standing Conference on Personal Service, printed in *Social Service
        Review*, Vol. xii, 1931, pp. 7-10. The 'personal service' movement
        had been founded by Violet Markham in the wake of the 1909
        Poor Law Commission to promote a more scientific and less class-
        oriented method of casework than that practised by the COS.

59 *Social Service Review*, Vol. xii, 1931, editorial on 'The crisis and after', pp. 173-74; Grundy, S.P., 'Social service and deflation', *ibid.*, pp. 183-84; Miss Hugh Smith, 'The future of social service', *Social Welfare*, Vol. ii, 1933, pp. 87-89.

60 Farquharson, A., 'Surveys and community life', report of an address to the annual conference of LePlay House *Sociological Review*, Vol. xxii, 1930, pp. 66-71.

61 One of the few persistent dissenters from this view was Harold Laski, who paradoxically was a strong supporter of state *economic* intervention. Idealist critics of Laski were not slow to pick upon this apparent contradiction in his thought: see the anonymous review of Laski's *Liberty in the Modern State*, in *Social Service Review*, Vol. xi, 1930, p. 243. I have not in this article discussed the political thought of pluralists and guild socialists, who shared the Idealist view that human groups had real corporate personalities while rejecting the emphasis of many Idealists on the transcendent status of the state.

62 Greenwood, 'Plea for voluntary service', *op. cit.*, p. 161.

63 Raven, A., 'Normal and abnormal psychology in relation to social welfare', *Sociological Review*, Vol. xxi, 1929, pp. 125-29.

64 Lindsay, A.D., 'Political theory', in Marvin, F.S. (ed.), *Recent Developments in European Thought*, Oxford: Oxford University Press, 1920, pp. 164-80. Lindsay was not wholly uncritical of theorists of the Idealist school, not on grounds of philosophic method, but because of their over-emphasis on the national state at the expense of other greater and lesser moral communities.

65 Seth, J. *English Philosophers and Schools of Philosophy*, London: J.M. Dent, 1912, pp. 358-67.

66 Lindsay, A.D., 'Philosophy as criticism of standards', paper to the Scots Philosophical Club, 29 September 1950, reprinted in his *Selected Addresses*, Cumberland: Holmrook, 1957, p. 150.

67 For example, Ford, P., 'Indices of social conditions in Southampton', *Sociological Review*, Vol. xxiii, 1931, pp. 22-33; Falk, W., 'The sociological interpretation of political ideas', *Sociological Review*, Vol. xxvi, 1934, pp. 268-87; Jahoda, M., 'Some ideas on social and psychological research', *Sociological Review*, Vol. xxx, 1938, pp. 63-80. It would of course be quite wrong to imply that there had been no such trends earlier: see Low, B., 'Civic ideals: some psycho-analytical considerations', *Sociological Review*, Vol. xiv, 1922, pp. 213-16.

68 For example, *The Youth Service in England and Wales*, London: HMSO, 1958. This report is of particular historical interest in this respect because it combined a strong commitment to organic and 'communitarian' values with a commentary on the growing

cultural and linguistic difficulty of articulating those values in the Britain of the late 1950s.

69   Harris, J., *William Beveridge: A Biography*, second edn., Oxford: Clarendon Press, 1997, pp. 484-88.

70   Titmuss, R.M., *Essays on the Welfare State*, London: Allen and Unwin, 1958; Titmuss, R.M., *Commitment to Welfare*, London: Allen and Unwin, 1968.

71   Gregory, R.A., 'The curriculum of the elementary school: reading, writing and arithmetic', in *Proceedings of the National Conference on the Prevention of Destitution*, pp. 167-75, 12 June 1912. See also Greenwood, A., 'The organisation of the juvenile labour market', *Progress*, No. 22, January 1911, p. 97.

72   Macadam, *Equipment of the Social Worker, op. cit.*, pp. 53-54. The introduction to Macadam's book was written by J.H. Muirhead, the Idealist professor of philosophy at Birmingham University.

73   Ainscow, E., 'State and parent: a co-operative partnership', *Social Welfare*, Vol. ii, 1934, pp. 99-103.

74   den Otter, ' Search for a "social philosophy" ', *op. cit.*, pp. 181-85.

75   Burns, E.M., *Ideas in Conflict: The Political Theories of the Contemporary World*, second edn., London: Methuen, 1963, pp. 254-55. Wiener, M., *English Culture and the Decline of the Industrial Spirit, 1850-1980*, Cambridge, 1981, does not deal specifically with philosophy, but includes in its critique many early twentieth-century theorists and public figures, such as Dean Inge and Ernest Barker, whose ideas link them closely with the Idealist school.

76   For a discussion of the problem in these terms, see Urwick, *Social Good, op. cit.*, p. 197: 'The underlying cause of the troubles is just this; that, in the Great Societies, *citizenship is not real*; it cannot operate as an effective reality; it cannot be felt as real'.

77   'Why is a stockbroker less beautiful than a Homeric warrior or an Egyptian priest? Because he is less Incorporated with life, he is not inevitable, but accidental, almost parasitic': Dawson, 'Progress and decay in ancient and modern civilization', *op. cit.*, p. 10.

78   Pigou, A.C., *Wealth and Welfare*, London: Macmillan, 1912; Hobson, J.A., 'Economic art and human welfare', *Journal of Philosophical Studies*, Vol. xxxvi, 1925-26, pp. 162-85.

A.W. Vincent

1   Rose, M. E., *The English Poor Law 1780-1930*, Newton Abbot, Devon: David and Charles, 1971, p. 266.

2   *Ibid.*, p. 266.

3   Finlayson, G., 'Penlee's appeal to philanthropy', *The Times Higher Education Supplement*, 23 April 1982, p. 13.

4   Barker, R., *Political Ideas in Modern Britain*, London: Methuen, 1978, p. 60; Rowntree, S., *The Poverty Line: A Reply*, London: Henry Good and Sons, 1901, p. 28; Webb, B., *My Apprenticeship*, London: Longman's, 1926, p. 206.

5   Briggs, A., *Social Thought and Social Action: A Study of the Work of Seebohm Rowntree 1871-1954*, London: Longman's, 1961. Similar views can be found in Gilberts, B.B., *The Evolution of National Insurance; The Origins of the Welfare State*, London: Michael Joseph, 1966, p. 52. In Mowat, C.L., *The Charity Organisation Society 1869-1913: Its Ideas and Work*, London: Methuen, 1961, p. 38, Mowat speaks of the COS as being imprisoned in a 'sternly individualist philosophy'. In Rimlinger, G.V., *Welfare Policy and Industrialisation in Europe, America and Russia*, New York: Wiley, 1971, p. 71, Rimlinger argues that 'The Charity Organisation Society represented the main effort of the free market society to solve the problem of poverty without government intervention'.

6   Briggs, *Social Thought and Social Action, op. cit.*, p. 20.

7   Beveridge, Lord, *Voluntary Action: A Report on Methods of Social Advance*, London: George Allen & Unwin, 1948, pp. 144-49; Bruce, M., *The Coming of the Welfare State*, London: B.T. Batsford, 1966, p. 106; Marshall, T.H., *Social Policy in the Twentieth Century*, London: Hutchinson, 1967, p. 167; Owen, D., *English Philanthropy 1660-1960*, London: Oxford University Press, 1965, p. 222; Rose, M., *The Relief of Poverty 1834-1914*, London: Macmillan, 1972, pp. 25-27; Pinker R., *Social Theory and Social Policy*, London: Heinemann, 1971, p. 82; Fraser, D., *The Evolution of the British Welfare State*, London: Macmillan, 1973, p. 121.

8   Marshall, p. 167; Owen, p. 216.

9   Rose, *Relief, op. cit.*, p. 26.

10 Stedman Jones, G., *Outcast London: A Study of the Relationship between Classes in Victorian Society*, Harmondsworth: Penguin, 1976, pp. 256-57.

11 *Ibid.*, p. 257.

12 Webb, B., *Our Partnership*, London: Longman's, 1948, p. 432.

13 Bosanquet, B., 'Charity Organisation and the Majority Report', *International Journal of Ethics*, 20, 1910, p. 395.

14 Mowat, *op. cit.*, pp. 160-61, 164.

15 Webb, *Our Partnership, op. cit.*, p. 452.

16 Bosanquet, H. and Bosanquet, B., 'Charity Organisation: A Reply', *Contemporary Review*, Vol. 71, 1897, p. 112.

17   Quoted in Rooff, M., *A Hundred Years of Family Welfare, a Study of the Family Welfare Association 1869-1970*, London: Michael Joseph, 1972, p. 35.

18   Bosanquet, B., *The Philosophical Theory of the State*, London: Macmillan, 1899.

19   Compare United Kingdom, Parliament, *Poor Laws and the Relief of Distress*, Command Papers, Cd. 4499, 1909.

20   Bosanquet, B., 'The Reports of the Poor Law Commission', *Sociological Review*, Vol. 2, No. 2, 1909.

21   Bosanquet, 'Charity Organisation', *op. cit.,* p. 399

22   United Kingdom, Parliament, *Poor Laws and the Relief of Distress*, Command Papers, Cd. 4499, 1909, p. 259.

23   Bosanquet, 'Reports', *op. cit.,* p. 114.

24   *Ibid.,* p. 114.

25   Compare Loch, C.S. (ed.), *Methods of Social Advance*, London: Macmillan, 1904, and Loch, C.S., 'Christianity and Social Questions', *Charity Organisation Review*, No. 86, 1904.

26   Cormack, U., *The Welfare State: The Royal Commission on the Poor Laws 1905-1909*, Loch Memorial Lecture, London: Family Welfare Association, 1953, p. 17.

27   Compare Bosanquet, B., 'Idealism in Social Work', *Charity Organisation Review*, No. 15, 1898; also Bosanquet, B., *Social and International Ideals*, London: Macmillan, 1917.

28   Bosanquet, 'Idealism in Social Work', *op. cit.,* p. 129.

29   Bosanquet, *Social and International Ideals, op. cit.,* p. 77.

30   Bosanquet, 'Idealism in Social Work', *op. cit.,* p. 124.

31   Compare Dendy, H. (later Bosanquet), 'Thorough charity', *Charity Organisation Review*, No. 101, 1893; see also Loch, C.S., 'The programme of the Charity Organisation Society', *Charity Organisation Review*, No. 163, 1910.

32   Bosanquet, 'Charity Organisation', *op. cit.,* p. 397.

33   Webb, *My Apprenticeship, op. cit.,* p. 206.

34   Pinker, *Social Theory and Social Policy, op. cit.,* pp. 29-30.

35   Compare Bosanquet, B., *The Civilisation of Christendom*, London: Swan Sonnenschein, 1899, p. 382.

36   Dendy, H., 'The industrial residuum', in Bosanquet, B. (ed.), *Aspects of the Social Problem*, London: Macmillan, 1895, p. 97.

37   Bosanquet, B., 'Charity Organisation', *op. cit.,* p. 397.

38   Bosanquet, B., 'The reality of the general will', *Aspects, op.cit.*, p. 322.

39   Hegel, G.W.F., *The Philosophy of Right*, trans. Knox, T.M., Oxford: Oxford University Press, 1971, para. four, addition, p. 226.

40   *Ibid.*, para. 21, p. 29.

41   Körner, S., *Kant*, Harmondsworth: Penguin, 1955, pp. 147-51.

42   Bradley, F.H., *Collected Essays*, Oxford: Clarendon Press, 1935, Vol. II, pp. 444-45; see also p. 476.

43   Bosanquet, B., 'The Reality', *Aspects, op. cit.*, p. 324.

44   *Ibid.*, p. 325.

45   Loch, C.S., *Charity Organisation and Social Life*, London: Macmillan, 1910, pp. 367-68.

46   Bosanquet, H., *The Strength of the People: A Study in Economics*, London: Macmillan, 1902, pp. 51-52.

47   Bosanquet, B., 'Reports', *op. cit.*, pp. 114-15.

48   Bosanquet, B., 'Charity Organisation', *op. cit.*, p. 400.

49   *Ibid.*, p. 405.

50   Webb, S., 'The end of the poor law', *Sociological Review*, Vol. 2, No. 2, 1909, pp. 127-39.

51   Webb, S. and Webb, B., *English Poor Law Policy*, London: Longman's 1911, p. 275.

52   Webb, S. and Webb, B., *The Prevention of Destitution*, London: Longman's, 1911, p. 9. Hereafter cited in the text as *Prevention*.

53   Webb and Webb, *English Poor Law Policy, op. cit.*, p. 351.

54   *Ibid.*, p. 360.

55   Webb, B., *Our Partnership, op. cit.*, p. 403.

56   Webb and Webb, *Prevention, op. cit.*, p. 293.

57   *Ibid.*, pp. 333-34.

58   Hobson, J.A., 'The social philosophy of charity organisation', *Contemporary Review*, Vol. 19, 1896, p. 720.

59   Bosanquet and Bosanquet, 'A reply', *op. cit.*, p. 115.

60   Muirhead, J.H., *By What Authority: The Principles in Common and at Issue in the Reports of the Poor Law Commission*, London: P.S. King and Son, 1909, p. 32.

61   Bosanquet, H., *The Standard of Life and Other Essays*, London: Macmillan, 1898, p. 37.

62   An interesting discussion of the issue of character is given in
      Collini, S., *Liberalism and Sociology: L.T. Hobhouse and Political
      Argument in England 1880-1914*, Cambridge: Cambridge
      University Press, 1979, p. 31. Collini calls the concept of
      character the Trojan Horse of Victorian social theory, and it is this
      concept which unknowingly facilitated the growth of certain
      collectivist ideas. This is precisely the point that I wish to make
      about the COS.

63   Bosanquet, H., *Social Work in London 1869-1912*, 1914, rpt. edn.,
      Brighton, Sussex: Harvester press, 1973, p. 190. The work of Jose
      Harris goes some way to confirming this point; see Harris, J.,
      Unemployment and Politics, London: Oxford University Press,
      1972, pp. 105-10.

64   Marshall, *Social Policy in the Twentieth Century, op. cit.*, p. 167.

65   Webb, B., *Our Partnership, op. cit.*, p. 97.

66   Webb and Webb, *Prevention, op. cit.*, p. 320.

67   Webb and Webb, *English Poor Law Policy, op. cit.*, p. 358.

68   Cormack, *The Welfare State: The Royal Commission on the Poor
      Laws 1905-1909, op. cit.*, p. 16.

Pat Thane

1   Pelling, H., 'The working class and the welfare state', in *Popular
      Politics and Society in Victorian Britain*, London: Macmillan, 1968.

2   Gilbert, B.B., *The Evolution of National Insurance in Great Britain*,
      London: Michael Joseph, 1966; Gosden, P.H.J.H., *Self-help:
      Voluntary Associations in Great Britain*, London: Batsford, 1973.

3   *Oddfellows Magazine*, October 1885, January 1886, August,
      September, October 1891, January 1893, January 1894, January
      1899, *Hearts of Oak Journal*, October 1902.

4   *Rechabite and Temperance Magazine*, March 1891.

5   *Foresters' Miscellany*, April 1897.

6   *Ibid.*, July 1896.

7   *Ibid.*, December 1894.

8   *Ibid.*

9   *Ibid.*, June 1894.

10   *Ibid.*, July 1896.

11   *Ibid.*, November 1895.

12   Gilbert, *The Evolution of National Insurance in Great Britain, op. cit.*,
      ch. 4.

13   *Foresters' Miscellany*, December 1891.

14   Ryan, P.A., 'Poplarism 1894-1930', in Thane, P. (ed.), *The Origins of British Social Policy*, London: Croom Helm, 1978.

15   And were being proposed by employers. See Hay R., 'Employers and social policy in Britain: the evolution of welfare legislation 1905-1914', *Social History*, Vol. iv, January 1977.

16   *Report of the Royal Commission on the Aged Poor*, C. 7684, 1895. Minutes of evidence, Q. 12, 342. Chamberlain, J., 'Old-age pensions', *National Review*, February 1892.

17   *Justice*, 12 April 1890.

18   *Ibid.*, 9 March, 18 May, 22 June 1889; 4 January, 11 January, 5 April, 12 April 1890 (*inter alia*).

19   *Ibid.*, 5 July 1890.

20   *Ibid.*, 5 April, 8 June, 5 July 1890; 2 February 1891.

21   *Ibid.*, 4 March, 18 May 1889; 24 March 1894.

22   *Ibid.*, 22 June 1889; 3 October 1896 (*inter alia*).

23   *Ibid.*, 16 July 1898.

24   Hyndman, H.M., *A Commune for London*, 1887.

25   *Justice*, 2 February, 22 June 1889; 8 June, 14 September 1890; 30 November 1895; 31 October 1896.

26   Hay, J. M., 'Industrial strife and business welfare philosophy', *Business History*, Vol. xxi, 1979; 'Non-commissioned officers: British employers and their supervisory workers', *Social History*, Vol. v, 1980; 'Employers, industrial housing and the evolution of company welfare policies in Britain's heavy industry', *International Review of Social History*, Vol. xxvi, 1981; Whiteside, N., 'Industrial labour, unemployment and the growth of social insurance 1900-1930', paper to the international economic history congress, Budapest, August 1982.

27   Whiteside, 'Industrial labour, unemployment and the growth of social insurance 1900-1930', *op. cit.*

28   'Fourth report of commissioners appointed to inquire into friendly and benefit building societies', Appendix xvi: Rules of the friendly societies in England and Scotland, *Parliamentary papers*, 1874, Vol. xxiii.

29   Phelps Brown, E.H., *The Growth of British Industrial Relations*, London: Macmillan, 1959, p. 224.

30   *Report of the Annual Conference of the TUC*, 1896, pp. 29-31.

31   *Ibid.*, 1890, pp. 27-29.

32   *Ibid.*, 1890, p. 27; 1894, p. 20; 1898, p. 25, pp. 30-31; 1902, p. 36; 1903, p. 36; 1899, p. 45.

33   Burgess, K., 'Working class response to social policy: the case of the Lancashire cotton textile districts 1880-1914', paper to the Social Science Research Council conference on social policy, University of Glasgow, May 1978.

34   *Ibid.*

35   Whiteside has begun this task.

36   Pelling, 'The working class and the welfare state', *op. cit.*, p. 18.

37   See, among others, Liverpool Trades Council, *Annual Reports*, 1888-89, 1894, 1896, 1901-02; Bradford Trades Council, *Annual Reports*, 1899, 1901, 1902, 1905; Leeds District Trades and Labour Council, *Annual Reports*, 1892, 1900, 1904, 1905; London Trades Council, *Annual Reports*, 1889, 1891, 1899, 1900, 1901, 1902; Bolton and District United Trades Council, *Annual Reports*, 1896, 1897; Birmingham Trades Council, *Annual Reports*, 1889, 1890, 1895, 1897, 1898, 1898, 1901, 1907, 1909; Clinton, A., 'Trades councils from the beginning of the 20th century to the Second World War', PhD., thesis, University of London, 1973, espec. ch. 3; and Clinton, A., *The Trade Union Rank and File*, 1977. On Bradford see Brockway, F., *Socialism Over Sixty Years—A Life of Jowitt of Bradford*, 1946; Cahill, M. and Jowitt, T., 'The new philanthropy: the emergence of the Bradford City Guild of Help', *Journal of Social Policy*, II, 1980.

38   Clinton, *The Trade Union Rank and File*, 1977.

39   Liverpool Trades Council, *Annual Report*, 1894.

40   Carlisle Trades Council, *Annual Report*, 1910.

41   Pelling, 'The working class and the welfare state', *op. cit.*, p. 10.

42   Stead, F.H., *How Old-Age Pensions Began To Be*, London: 1910; Rogers, F., *Ten Years Work for Old-Age Pensions*, London: 1909 and *Labour, Life and Literature*, London: 1913; *Annual Reports and Balance Sheets NCOL*, 1899-1909, Williams (Thane), P.M., 'The development of old-age pensions in the UK 1878-1925', Ph.D. Thesis, University of London, 1970.

43   *Second and Third Annual Reports and Balance Sheets NCOL*, 1900 and 1901.

44   *Third Annual Report and Balance Sheet NCOL*, 1901.

45   *Ibid.*, 1904.

46   Introduction to Englander, D. (ed.), *The Diary of Fred Knee*, Oxford: Society for the Study of Labour History, Bulletin Supplement, Aids to Research No. 3, Coventry, 1977.

47   *Housing Journal,* August 1900, March 1901, September 1901, October 1901, February 1904, February, March, June 1905, April, July 1906, January 1906.

48   *Ibid.,* March 1901.

49   *Ibid.,* January 1901.

50   *Ibid.,* March 1901.

51   *Ibid.,* August 1901.

52   Brown, K.D., *Labour and Unemployment,* Newton Abbot: David & Charles, 1971; Harris, J., *Unemployment and Politics 1886-1914,* Oxford: Oxford University Press, 1972, chs., II and V.

53   Pollard, S., 'The foundation of the co-operative party', in Briggs, A. and Saville, J. (eds.), *Essays in Labour History,* London: Macmillan, 1971; *Co-operative Congress Reports,* 1890, p. 12; 1891, p. iii; 1892, pp. 55, 65, 115-121.

54   *Co-operative Congress Report,* 1890, pp. 12ff.

55   Women's Co-operative Guild, *Annual Reports,* 1893-1914.

56   *Ibid.,* 1897, 1901, 1902.

57   *The Extension of Co-operation to the Poor,* report of an enquiry by the Women's Co-operative Guild, London, 1902, p. 19.

58   *Labour Leader,* 13 March, 29 May 1908.

59   Massingham, H.W., 'The Newcastle programme', *Labour Leader,* 10 October, 31 October, 21 November 1891.

60   *Ibid.,* 28 November 1891.

61   *Labour Leader,* 10 October, 17 October, 24 October, 14 November, 12 December 1891; 22 November 1907; 31 January, 7 February, 13 March, 20 March, 12 April 1908; 27 January, 3 February, 17 February 1911.

62   Leading articles in *Labour Leader,* 17 October, 28 November 1891.

63   *Ibid.,* 7 November, 28 November, 5 December 1891; 20 January, 12 May 1911.

64   *Ibid.,* 10 October, 17 October, 28 November, 5 December 1891; 17 January, 13 March 1908.

65   Russell, A.K., *Liberal Landslide,* Newton Abbot: David & Charles, 1973, pp. 65-83.

66   Barker, R., *Education and Politics 1900-51: A Study of the Labour Party,* Oxford: Oxford University Press, 1972.

67   Minutes of a London school board 1871, quoted in Rubinstein, D., *School Attendance in London 1870-1904,* Hull: 1969, p. 84.

68   Rubinstein, *School Attendance in London 1870-1904, op. cit.,* p. 13ff.

69   *Ibid.,* p. 62.

70   *Ibid.,* p. 91.

71   *Ibid.,* pp. 90-91.

72   Pelling, 'The working class and the welfare state', *op. cit.,* pp. 2-6.

73   Thane, P., 'Contributory vs. non-contributory pensions 1878-1908', in Thane (ed.), *Origins of British Social Policy, op. cit.,*

74   Lewis, J., *The Politics of Motherhood,* London: Croom Helm, 1980, pp. 18-20.

75   Joslin, D. and Winter, J. (eds.), *R.H. Tawney's Commonplace Book,* Cambridge: Cambridge University Press, 1972, pp. 3-4.

76   Hay, J.R., *The Origins of the Liberal Welfare Reforms 1906-14,* London: Macmillan, 1975, p. 28; Yeo, S., 'Working class association, private capital, welfare and the state in the late 19th and 20th centuries', in Parry, N., Rustin, M. and Satyamurti, C., *Social Work, Welfare and the State,* 1977, pp. 70-71.

77   Reynolds, S., Woolley, Bob and Woolley, T., *Seems So! A Working Class View of Politics,* 1911, p. 328.

78   *Ibid.,* p. 178.

79   Wright, H. (ed.)., *Letters of Stephen Reynolds,* 1923, p. 142.

80   Reynolds, Woolley and Woolley, *Seems So!, op. cit.,* p. 329.

81   Pelling, 'The working class and the welfare state', *op. cit.,* p. 19.

82   *Foresters' Miscellany,* February 1903; October 1904; April, July, September 1907; Williams, 'The development of old-age pensions in the UK 1878-1925', *op. cit.,* p. 167.

83   Gilbert, *The Evolution of National Insurance in Great Britain, op. cit.,* pp. 109-11.

84   *Justice,* 19 August 1890; Clinton,'Trades councils from the beginning of the 20th century to the Second World War', *op. cit.,* p. 84; Women's Co-operative Guild, *Annual Report,* 1903.

85   Thane,'Contributory vs. non-contributory pensions 1878-1908', *op. cit.,* pp. 99 -104; Williams, 'The development of old-age pensions in the UK 1878-1925', *op. cit.* pp. 200-35; *Ninth Annual Report and Balance Sheet,* NCOL, 1908.

86   Thompson, F., *Lark Rise,* Oxford: Oxford University Press, 1940, p. 100.

87 *The Times*, 12 May 1908; Williams, 'The development of old-age pensions in the UK 1878-1925', *op. cit.*, p. 218.

88 Liverpool Trades Council minutes, 13 May 1908.

89 Hay R., 'Employers and social policy in Britain: the evolution of welfare legislation 1905-1914', *op. cit.*, pp. 442-53.

90 For discussion of Labour's contribution to the making and timing of these measures see Saville, J., 'The welfare state: an historical approach', *New Reasoner*, Vol. 1, No. 3, pp. 5-25; Dorothy Thompson's reply, *New Reasoner*, Vol. 1, No. 4, pp. 128-29; and the comments by Hay, *Origins of the Liberal Welfare Reforms, op. cit.*, pp. 25-29.

91 Brown, *Labour and Unemployment, op. cit.*, pp. 144-60.

92 *League Leaflet*, January 1911. Harris, *Unemployment and Politics 1886-1914, op. cit.*, pp. 317-18, 329-30, 354.

93 *Report of the Royal Commission on the Aged Poor*, C. 7684, 1895. Minutes of evidence, QQ. 16, 926-28. *Report of the Select Committee on the Aged Deserving Poor*, 1899, evidence of G. Tuckwell.

94 *League Leaflet*, January, March, April, May-November 1912; January-May 1913; *Labour Woman*, January 1914.

95 *Labour Leader*, 1 March, 5 April 1907.

96 *League Leaflet*, March 1913.

97 *Daily Herald* leader, 'The great employers' act', 12 September 1912.

98 Lansbury, G., 'Socialists and socialism', *Daily Herald*, 13 January 1913.

99 *Daily Herald* leader, 'The great employers' act', 12 September 1912.

100 Harris, *Unemployment and Politics 1886-1914, op. cit.*, p. 354.

101 *Daily Herald*, 29 June, 10 July, 14 August 1912.

102 Clinton, 'Trades councils from the beginning of the 20th century to the Second World War', *op. cit.*, pp. 94-95.

103 TUC, *Annual Reports*, 1909, pp. 155-57; 1910, pp. 191-92; Whiteside, 'Industrial labour, unemployment and the growth of social insurance 1900-1930', *op. cit.*, p. 10.

104 Harris, *Unemployment and Politics 1886-1914, op. cit.*, ch. vi; Whiteside, 'Industrial labour, unemployment and the growth of social insurance 1900-1930', *op. cit.*, p. 10.

105 A TUC special conference on labour exchanges held in 1909
supported them 'provided that the management boards contain an
equal proportion of employers and representatives of trade
unions'. TUC *Report*, 1909, p. 54; *League Leaflet*, March 1912;
Whiteside, 'Industrial labour, unemployment and the growth of
social insurance 1900-1930', *op. cit.*, p. 10; Harris, *Unemployment
and Politics 1886-1914, op. cit.*, pp. 354-55.

138

Index